Early praise for *Web Development with ReasonML*

By the time of the book's conclusion, the reader will not only have become familiar with a new language's syntax and semantics in isolation, but will have learned how to integrate it with other familiar tools and frameworks like React and webpack to build a modest web application. In other words, the reader will walk away armed not only with a paradigmatic shift in their thinking towards a functional style of programming, but also with the skills required to put it to practical use in their daily work.

➤ **Arno Bastenhof**
   Solution Architect, Rabobank

An authoritative and comprehensive introduction to ReasonML. I definitely learned a lot and look forward to finding excuses to use it in a new application.

➤ **Peter Hampton**
   Senior Software Developer, Citi

Finally, a complete path for learning how to be a functional programmer for the web with ReasonML and React. The author incrementally builds upon what you've created in the previous chapters. When you complete the book, you'll have all the elements needed to start to work with ReasonML by yourself.

➤ **Massimiliano Bertinetti**
   Full-Stack Developer, Softwave Soluzioni e Tecnologie

This is great book for people who want to learn ReasonML properly.

➤ **Riza Fahmi**
Developer Evangelist, Co-Founder, HACKTIV8

Even though ReasonML is still young, there are already plenty of success stories of organizations adopting it to become more productive. J. David Eisenberg has put together the best starter manual on ReasonML. Anyone who wants access to build more robust web applications using ReasonML's powerful toolchain should definitely give this a read.

➤ **Lewis Chung**
CTO, ShopWith

Web Development with ReasonML

Type-Safe, Functional Programming for JavaScript Developers

J. David Eisenberg

The Pragmatic Bookshelf

Raleigh, North Carolina

Many of the designations used by manufacturers and sellers to distinguish their products are claimed as trademarks. Where those designations appear in this book, and The Pragmatic Programmers, LLC was aware of a trademark claim, the designations have been printed in initial capital letters or in all capitals. The Pragmatic Starter Kit, The Pragmatic Programmer, Pragmatic Programming, Pragmatic Bookshelf, PragProg and the linking *g* device are trademarks of The Pragmatic Programmers, LLC.

Every precaution was taken in the preparation of this book. However, the publisher assumes no responsibility for errors or omissions, or for damages that may result from the use of information (including program listings) contained herein.

Our Pragmatic books, screencasts, and audio books can help you and your team create better software and have more fun. Visit us at *https://pragprog.com.*

The team that produced this book includes:

Publisher: Andy Hunt
VP of Operations: Janet Furlow
Managing Editor: Susan Conant
Development Editor: Andrea Stewart
Copy Editor: Sean Dennis
Indexing: Potomac Indexing, LLC
Layout: Gilson Graphics

For sales, volume licensing, and support, please contact *support@pragprog.com.*

For international rights, please contact *rights@pragprog.com.*

ISBN-13: 978-1-68050-633-4
Book version: P1.0—March 2019

Contents

Introduction

JavaScript has taken its place as a major programming language. It seems to be everywhere, has a large, flourishing ecosystem, and works both client- and server-side. It has effectively become a *lingua franca* for the Web. At the same time that JavaScript has grown, two trends in programming have grown in popularity for front-end web development: functional programming and static typing. Functional programming helps you avoid the problems that come with mutable data and mutable global state. Static typing moves many programming errors from runtime to compile time so your program's users never encounter them.

The result of this convergence has been the creation of functional programming libraries such as Lodash,[1] tools like Flow[2] that help with static typing, and functional, statically typed languages that compile to JavaScript, such as TypeScript,[3] PureScript,[4] Elm,[5] and ReasonML.[6]

What Makes ReasonML Special?

With all these choices, why choose ReasonML? First, ReasonML is not a new language that compiles to JavaScript. Rather, it is a new syntax for OCaml, an established language used in industry for over 20 years. With ReasonML, you get OCaml's strong static-type system with an excellent type inference engine as well as its features for functional programming with immutable variables.

For those times when you need to break away from the functional world, ReasonML allows "opt-in side-effect, mutation and object[s] for familiarity &

---

1. lodash.com/
2. flow.org/
3. www.typescriptlang.org/
4. www.purescript.org/
5. elm-lang.org/
6. reasonml.github.io/

interop[eration with JavaScript], while keeping the rest of the language pure, immutable and functional."[7] ReasonML hits the sweet spot between the purely theoretical world and the laissez-faire approach of JavaScript, but always with the emphasis on getting things done.

ReasonML's syntax has been designed to be familiar to JavaScript programmers, with features that let you create bindings to existing JavaScript libraries. The compilation is incredibly fast, and the code ReasonML produces is highly readable. You aren't restricted to compiling to JavaScript—because ReasonML is OCaml, you can also compile to native code.

There are combinations of languages and libraries that give you all these capabilities, but ReasonML has them all—it's a "one-stop shop" for your programming needs, and that's why it's special.

What Should You Know?

We're going to presume that you have some experience programming in JavaScript. On the client side, you are familiar with HTML and CSS and have some knowledge of programming the Document Object Model (DOM). It's useful but not necessary to have experience with a framework like React or Vue.

What's in This Book?

In Chapter 1, Make Your First ReasonML Project, on page 1, you'll learn to set up your system to compile and run short programs using variables, built-in data types, and operations on numbers and strings.

Chapter 2, Writing Functions, on page 15 shows you how to write functions as you learn more about ReasonML's type inference. You'll also learn about currying, which allows you to apply only some of a function's arguments to create a new function.

In Chapter 3, Creating Your Own Data Types, on page 29, you'll be able to create your own data types which automatically take advantage of ReasonML's type inference engine. You'll also learn about the option data type, which ensures that your code handles both cases of an operation that may or may not succeed. This helps you avoid the dreaded null or undefined errors at run time.

Chapter 4, Interacting with Web Pages, on page 47 will have you creating web pages that call on ReasonML code. You'll use the bs-webapi library to directly manipulate the DOM.

---

7.   reasonml.github.io/docs/en/what-and-why.html

In Chapter 5, Using Collections, on page 61, you'll work with tuples, lists, and arrays, and find out how to use the map(), keep(), and reduce() functions to transform the data in these collections without needing loops.

While map(), keep(), and reduce() are powerful and useful, sometimes you need to customize the iteration through a collection. In Chapter 6, Repeating with Recursion, on page 89, you will see how recursion lets you do this customization quite elegantly. You will also find out how the use of a technique called tail recursion lets ReasonML optimize the JavaScript it produces for best performance.

In Chapter 7, Structuring Data with Records and Modules, on page 103, you'll learn to construct data types with multiple fields and values, much like (but not identical to) JavaScript objects. You'll also explore how the use of modules lets you avoid name collisions between fields of different record types.

Chapter 8, Connecting to JavaScript, on page 119 returns to the world of JavaScript, showing you how to write bindings to existing JavaScript libraries so that they can be used in your ReasonML code. This is where you'll see how to deal with JavaScript objects.

Continuing further into JavaScript, Chapter 9, Making Applications with Reason/React, on page 141 shows you how to use the React framework with ReasonML to build a basic single-page web application. You'll see that ReasonML has been designed to integrate well with React.

Acknowledgments

Thanks to Andrea Stewart, a great editor.

Thanks also to the people who contributed to OpenClipArt.org:[8]

- Cell phone in Chapter 2, Writing Functions, on page 15 by user lifeincolour, keypad by user Startright

- Icons in Chapter 9, Making Applications with Reason/React, on page 141 by user sixsixfive

- Animal drawings by users scout, deb53, juhele, and davidblyons

- Graphics for recursive drawing in Chapter 6, Repeating with Recursion, on page 89 by users Arvin61r58, DooFi, Firkin, gnokii, and tomas_arad

Special thanks to the technical reviewers who made many useful and insightful suggestions: Arno Bastenhof, Massimiliano Bertinetti, Eduard Bondarenko,

---

8. openclipart.org/

Lewis Chung, Sam Elliott, Riza Fahmi, Avi Goel, Peter Hampton, Luca Mezzalira, Nick McGinness, António Monteiro, Khoa Nguyen, Carmelo Piccione, Kristof Semjen, and Gianluigi Spagnuolo. Thanks go to all the people who noted errata in the beta versions of this book, especially Peer Reynders for his many excellent comments. Also, thanks to the people in the Discord chat rooms who answered my many naïve questions.

Online Resources

You can download all the example source code for this book from its Pragmatic Bookshelf website.[9] You can also provide feedback by submitting errata entries.

If you're reading the book in PDF form, you can click the link above a code listing to view or download the specific examples.

Ready to get started? Great—let's begin.

---

9. pragprog.com/book/reasonml/

CHAPTER 1

Make Your First ReasonML Project

This is the introductory chapter and, as with most such chapters, its main purpose is to give you a quick start with ReasonML and let you become comfortable with editing, compiling, and running ReasonML programs. The programs themselves are of limited interest—there's only so much charm in the phrase "Hello, world," and doing simple arithmetic isn't particularly exciting.

On the other hand, the things you'll learn from these programs are quite interesting. In the process of writing programs that use variables and operations on numbers and strings, we'll introduce you to one of ReasonML's main features: its type system. You'll see how ReasonML automatically ensures at compile time that operators work only with operands of the proper type. This makes it easier to write robust code, because type errors which would have happened at runtime are now caught before your program even has an opportunity to run. You'll also learn how to annotate your programs to make the typing explicit. Let's get started.

Running Your First Program

In this first section, we'll go through the steps involved in installing ReasonML, creating a project, and building and running the code.

Installing ReasonML

The ReasonML compiler takes your code and translates it to OCaml's abstract syntax tree (AST)—the intermediate stage of compilation. The AST code can be compiled into native code or JavaScript. In this book, we're focusing on JavaScript. The task of translating to JavaScript is handled by the Buckle-Script compiler, which produces (surprisingly readable) JavaScript code. You can get ReasonML and BuckleScript by installing bs-platform (the bs in bs-platform stands for BuckleScript), and the easiest way to do this is to use a package manager like npm[1] or Yarn.[2] In either case, you will need to have Node.js®[3] (which comes with npm).

```
npm install -g bs-platform
```

or

```
yarn global add bs-platform
```

bs-platform and a plain old text editor is enough to get you going, but you'd do well to visit reasonml.github.io/docs/en/installation and follow the instructions there to get tools and plugins for whichever editor you're currently using. This will make your life ever so much easier.

The ReasonML Ecosystem

 In case you are wondering what OCaml and BuckleScript are and what they're doing in a book about ReasonML, you'll find the answer in Appendix 1, Understanding the ReasonML Ecosystem, on page 169.

Creating a Project

Create a directory for your projects and a new project named first-project with commands like these:

```
you@computer:~> mkdir book-projects
you@computer:~> cd book-projects
you@computer:~/book-projects> bsb -init first-project -theme basic-reason
Making directory first-project
Symlink bs-platform in /home/you/book-projects/first-project
you@computer:~/book-projects>
```

The -theme option creates a template for a basic ReasonML program. The directory created by -init will look like this:

```
first-project
├── bsconfig.json
├── node_modules
│   └── bs-platform -> /path/to/.node/lib/node_modules/bs-platform
├── package.json
├── README.md
└── src
    └── Demo.re
```

---

1. www.npmjs.com/get-npm
2. yarnpkg.com/en/docs/install
3. nodejs.org/en/

File bsconfig.json contains configuration information about our project. It will become important later on. bs-platform is a symbolic link to the global bs-platform that we installed earlier. File package.json contains information that npm uses. README.md contains a standard set of instructions about building and running the program. The *pièce de résistance* is Demo.re, which, at this point, contains:

```
Js.log("Hello, BuckleScript and Reason!");
```

Yes, it's the infamous "Hello, world!" example, customized for ReasonML. There are things to be gleaned from even this short example:

- By convention, ReasonML uses the .re extension to indicate a ReasonML source file.

- The Js.log() function writes to your terminal (in Node) and to the web console for web apps.

- Strings are enclosed in double quotes. Unlike JavaScript, you can't use single quotes—we'll cover that in more detail in Working with Strings, on page 10.

- ReasonML requires a semicolon at the end of a statement to separate it from the next one. Here, we have only one statement, so we could omit this semicolon. But it doesn't hurt to keep it.

You can change the file name if you wish. For now, we'll keep it as it is. You can also add as many other .re files as you wish in your src directory. We'll discuss this further in Chapter 7, Structuring Data with Records and Modules, on page 103.

Building and Running the Program

Now let's build the project. We have to be in the project directory, so our first command will be to change to that directory. If you want to build the project one time only, do npm run build. If you want to set things up to rebuild your project every time you change the source file, do npm run start. Here's what npm run build looks like. The command invokes the bsb (BuckleScript build) program:

```
you@computer:~/book_projects> cd first_project
you@computer:~/book_projects/first_project> npm run build

> first-project@0.1.0 build /home/you/book-projects/first-project
> bsb -make-world

ninja: Entering directory `lib/bs'
[3/3] Building src/Demo.mlast.d
[1/1] Building src/Demo-Firstproject.cmj
```

If you're using Yarn, you build the code with the command yarn build.

This creates a JavaScript file named Demo.bs.js in the src directory. Then, in the same terminal window (or a different one if you're using npm run start), run the program:

```
you@computer:~/book-projects/first-project> node src/Demo.bs.js
Hello, BuckleScript and Reason!
```

Using Variables and Doing Arithmetic in ReasonML

Now that you know your way around compiling and running a program, let's create a program that uses variables and performs calculations. Specifically, we'll write a program that calculates a total price, given a quantity and per-unit price. From this point on, we'll be using examples from the code samples accompanying this book, downloadable from the Pragmatic Programmers website.

```
first-project/src/TotalPrice.re
let qty = 7;
let price = 15;
let total = qty * price;
Js.log2("The total price is $", total);
```

This code introduces variables. Variable names in ReasonML, like those in many other programming languages, must begin with a lowercase letter and may be followed by letters, digits, single quotes, and underscores. Variable names are case-sensitive.

Different from variables in other languages, where a variable is a reference to a location in memory where the data resides and can be modified at will, variables in ReasonML more closely resemble variables in algebra. In algebra, when you say $x = 6$, this binds the symbol x to the value 6. Wherever you have a 6, you can substitute x. Wherever you have x, you can substitute 6. You can't just change your mind in the middle of a proof and say $x = 7$.

Similarly, ReasonML variables are *immutable*. Once you bind a symbol to a value, you can't change it. To make the difference from other programming languages clear, this book uses *bind* instead of *set* or *assign*.

It is possible to write code like this:

```
let x = 6;
let x = 7;
Js.log(x);
```

This code won't generate any errors and will output a 7. Are we confused about immutable variables? Nope. When we write let x = 7; ReasonML creates a new binding of the same name x, which *shadows* the previous binding (which is no longer accessible). There are places where shadowing a variable can lead to more readable code, but using it to simulate mutability is considered to be very bad practice. Don't do it! ReasonML is designed to work well with immutable variables. (We'll investigate how to do mutability correctly—when you absolutely need it—in Working with Mutable Variables, on page 137.)

In our example code, the symbol qty is bound to the value 7, price to 15, and total to whatever qty * price works out to.

The Js.log2() function writes the values of its arguments to the console. There are Js.log3() and Js.log4() as well. ReasonML doesn't have functions with a non-fixed number of arguments, so we need these functions when we want to write two, three, or four items to the console. When we run the program, we get this:

```
you@computer:/path/to/code/first-project> node src/TotalPrice.bs.js
The total price is $ 105
```

Instead of using Js.log2(), why didn't we write something similar to what we would do in JavaScript:

```
Js.log("The total price is $" ++ total);
```

Two reasons: First, we haven't gotten to Working with Strings, on page 10 to discuss string concatenation with ++. And second, we're attempting to concatenate a string and an integer. In JavaScript, "The total price is $" + total automatically converts the integer to a string. ReasonML doesn't—it's very particular about making sure that operators are only used with operands of the correct types. This helps avoid the unpleasant surprises you can get in a dynamically typed language when you give an operand of the wrong type and the system "helpfully" does a conversion for you when the program runs.

Working with Types

To see an example of ReasonML's attention to detail about types, let's modify the preceding price calculation program to handle prices that aren't integers, such as $14.50. If we change the code to read:

```
let qty = 7;
let price = 14.50;
let total = qty * price;
Js.log2("The total price is $", total);
```

We get this compile error:

```
We've found a bug for you!
/path/to/code/first-project/src/FloatPrice.re 3:19-23

1 │ let qty = 7;
2 │ let price = 14.50;
3 │ let total = qty * price;
4 │ Js.log2("The total price is $", total);

This has type:
  float
But somewhere wanted:
  int

You can convert a float to a int with int_of_float.
If this is a literal, you want a number without a trailing dot (e.g. 20).
```

The 3:19-23 in the error message means that the error is in line 3, characters 19 through 23. On your terminal, you'll see that part of the line highlighted in the section of code following the error message.

ReasonML is a typed language, and its type inference engine has figured out that we're trying to multiply an integer by a float. But why is it insisting that we convert the float value 14.50 to an integer? Because we used the * operator, which is the *integer* multiplication operator. If we want to multiply floats, we need the *. operator. This is as good a time as any to give a summary of the integer and floating point arithmetic operators:

Operation	Integer	Float
Addition	+	+.
Subtraction	-	-.
Multiplication	*	*.
Division	/	/.
Remainder	mod	
Exponentiation		**

We want to multiply by 14.50, so we must use the *. operator, and both operands must be float.

first-project/src/FloatPrice.re
```
let qty = 7.0;
let price = 14.50;
let total = qty *. price;
Js.log2("The total price is $", total);
```

That produces this output:

```
you@computer:/path/to/code/first-project> node src/FloatPrice.bs.js
The total price is $ 101.5
```

Converting and Annotating Types

The error message we received in the preceding program was You can convert a float to a int with int_of_float. int_of_float is one of several data type conversion functions built into ReasonML. They were originally from BuckleScript/OCaml, so underscores are used to separate the words. THus, int_of_float(14.50) returns the integer 14. The decimal part is truncated—int_of_float(14.99) also returns 14. float_of_int(7) will convert its integer argument to 7.0.

Naming Variables

 The naming convention from OCaml and BuckleScript is to use underscores to separate words in a multi-word variable name. The naming convention for ReasonML follows the JavaScript lower camel case convention where each word is capitalized. In OCaml or BuckleScript, you might see a variable named age_in_years. In ReasonML, you'd write it as ageInYears. Again, this is the convention. If you decide to use underscores in ReasonML, the compiler won't complain. We can't make any promises about the people who read your code, though.

ReasonML does a very good job of figuring out your data types. You *can* add type specifications when you bind a variable by following its name with a colon and its data type. In this fully annotated version of the price program, we have returned qty to an integer and used float_of_int() to convert it for the multiplication:

first-project/src/TypedPrice.re
```
let qty: int = 7;
let price: float = 14.50;
let total: float = float_of_int(qty) *. price;
Js.log2("The total price is $", total);
```

But just because you can do something doesn't mean you should. Programmers rarely give explicit type annotations to individual variables in ReasonML code. In this book, you'll occasionally see variables explicitly typed in order to make a point clear. It's more common to see function definitions annotated, as described on page 22.

More About Math

The sqrt() function, and trigonometric functions such as sin(), cos(), and tan(), are available directly through the automatically imported Pervasives module.[4] That lets us write things like this:

```
let result = sqrt(abs_float(-3.75));
```

For any functions or constants that aren't available in Pervasives, you can access JavaScript's Math methods via the Js.Math library:[5]

```
let r = 7.0;
let area = Js.Math._PI *. r *. r;
```

Why the Underscore?

In ReasonML, if a name begins with a lowercase letter or underscore, it's a variable. If it begins with an uppercase letter, it's a module name. The authors of the Js.Math module wanted to use the famliar convention of using all capital letters for constants like PI and E. This required putting in the leading underscore to allow ReasonML to parse these constants as variable bindings.

If you're compiling ReasonML to native code, the Js.Math module isn't available to you. You'll have to to stick with Pervasives, as they're built into OCaml.

Doing Conditional Computation

Let's add a bit of complexity to our price calculator: discounts. If you order fewer than ten items, you get a 5% discount. Otherwise, you get a 10% discount. We want the program to:

1. Calculate the total price.

2. Calculate the appropriate discount rate.

3. Calculate the cost with and without discount.

4. Print both, properly labeled.

Step 2 requires us to use an if/else expression:

---

4.   reasonml.github.io/api/Pervasives.html

5.   bucklescript.github.io/bucklescript/api/Js.Math.html

first-project/src/DiscountPrice.re
```
let discount =
  if (qty < 10) {
    0.05;
  } else {
    0.10;
  };
```

In ReasonML, the if keyword introduces an *expression*, not a statement. This crucial difference means you can bind the result of an if expression to a variable. It also means you must provide an else clause, and the results of both clauses must be of the same type. The following two if expressions will cause compile errors. We're also introducing ReasonML *comments*, enclosed in /* and */.

```
/* Missing else clause */
let bad1 = if (qty < 10) { 0.05; };

/* if yields integer; else yields float */
let bad2 = if (qty < 10) {
  0;
} else {
  0.05;
};
```

The Case of the Missing else Keyword

In actuality, if you leave out the else clause, as in:

```
let bad1 = if (qty < 10) { 0.05; }
```

ReasonML provides one for you, yielding a special value known as *unit*, which we will see more of when we discuss writing functions on page 19. The preceding code is the same as:

```
let bad1 = if (qty < 10) {
  0.05
} else {
  ()
}
```

The compiler will complain with a type error, because float and unit are not the same type.

Even when your if clause yields unit, don't leave out the else clause because ReasonML programmers always expect to see it.

Here's the complete discounted price program:

first-project/src/DiscountPrice.re
```
let qty = 7;

let price = 14.50;

let discount =
  if (qty < 10) {
    0.05;
  } else {
    0.10;
  };

let total = float_of_int(qty) *. price;

let afterDiscount = total *. (1.0 -. discount);

Js.log2("Price before discount: $", total);
Js.log2("Price after discount: $", afterDiscount);
```

And its output:

```
> node src/DiscountPrice.bs.js
Price before discount: $ 101.5
Price after discount: $ 96.425
```

Along with the less than operator <, ReasonML supports the comparison operators <=, >, >=, ==, and !=.

All these operators yield values of type bool, which has two possible values: true and false. Operations on bool values are && (and), || (or), and ! (not).

If you have a simple if/else, such as the one in the discount program, you can use the *ternary operator* instead. It does the same thing as if/else, but you don't have to type as much:

```
let discount = (qty < 10) ? 0.05 : 0.10;
```

Working with Strings

The last data type we'll take up in this introduction is strings. Multi-character strings are enclosed in double quotes, and the ++ operator concatenates strings. Consider this statement:

```
let str = "door" ++ "bell"; /* binds value "doorbell" to variable str */
```

Back in the discussion of output for the program on page 5, we noted that code such as the example below doesn't compile properly because ++ requires both its operands to be strings. The variable total is float, and the compiler will complain bitterly:

```
let total = float_of_int(qty) *. price;

let afterDiscount = total *. (1.0 -. discount);

Js.log("Price before discount: $" ++ total ++ ".");
Js.log("Price after discount: $" ++ afterDiscount ++ ".");
```

```
 We've found a bug for you!
  /path/to/code/first-project/src/BadConcatDiscount.re 17:38-42

  15 │ let afterDiscount = total *. (1.0 -. discount);
  16 │
  17 │ Js.log("Price before discount: $" ++ total ++ ".");
  18 │ Js.log("Price after discount: $" ++ afterDiscount ++ ".");

 This has type:
   float
 But somewhere wanted:
   string
```

You can convert a float to a string with string_of_float.

With our newfound knowledge of ReasonML's type system, the last line of the error message tells us exactly how to fix the problem by using string_of_float() to convert the float to a string (there's also a string_of_int() function for converting integers to strings):

first-project/src/ConcatDiscount.re
```
Js.log("Price before discount: $" ++ string_of_float(total)  ++ ".");
Js.log("Price after discount: $" ++ string_of_float(afterDiscount) ++ ".");
```

This produces the desired output:

```
> node src/ConcatDiscount.bs.js
Price before discount: $101.5.
Price after discount: $96.425.
```

Characters vs. Strings

ReasonML also has character variables that contain exactly one character enclosed in single quotes:

```
let ch = 'Y';
```

This data type isn't commonly used in ReasonML programs because JavaScript, which is the most common target language for ReasonML, doesn't distinguish between one-character and multi-character strings.

ReasonML provides many functions in the Js.String library.[6] These functions correspond to the JavaScript String functions.[7] Here are a few of the function calls, using a string variable str:

JavaScript	ReasonML
str.length	Js.String.length(str)
str.toUpperCase	Js.String.toUpperCase(str)
str.indexOf("Reason")	Js.String.indexOf("Reason", str)

Working with Unicode

Let's translate the price program to French and run it:

first-project/src/BadUnicode.re
```
let qty = 7;

let price = 14.50;

let discount =
  if (qty < 10) {
    0.05;
  } else {
    0.10;
  };

let total = float_of_int(qty) *. price;

let afterDiscount = total *. (1.0 -. discount);

Js.log("Prix avant réduction: " ++ string_of_float(total)
  ++ " €");
Js.log("Prix après réduction: " ++ string_of_float(afterDiscount)
  ++ " €");
```

```
> node src/BadUnicode.bs.js
Prix avant rÃ©duction: 101.5â ¬
Prix aprÃ¨s rÃ©duction: 96.425â ¬
```

The output isn't what we expected. In ReasonML, strings in double quotes are evaluated as ASCII, whereas JavaScript evaluates them as Unicode. The solution is to use the delimiters {js|...|js} that tell ReasonML to evaluate the strings as Unicode:

first-project/src/Unicode.re
```
Js.log({js|Prix avant réduction: |js} ++ string_of_float(total)
  ++ {js| €|js});
Js.log({js|Prix après réduction: |js} ++ string_of_float(afterDiscount)
  ++ {js| €|js});
```

---

6.   bucklescript.github.io/bucklescript/api/Js.String.html

7.   developer.mozilla.org/en-US/docs/Web/JavaScript/Reference/Global_Objects/String

```
> node src/Unicode.bs.js
Prix avant réduction: 101.5 €
Prix après réduction: 96.425 €
```

And voilà—we get the output we want. The {js|...|js} notation also allows multi-line strings:

first-project/src/Poem.re

```
let poem = {js|The boy stood on the burning deck,
  Whence all but he had fled;
The flames that lit the battle's wreck...|js};

Js.log(poem);
```

We can also interpolate variables into a string by using the {j|...|j} notation with a $ before variable names to be interpolated:

first-project/src/Interpolation.re

```
Js.log({j|Prix avant réduction: $total €|j});
Js.log({j|Prix après réduction: $afterDiscount €|j});
```

It's Your Turn

Write a program that calculates wind chill. Given an air temperature T in degrees Celsius and a wind velocity V in kilometers per hour, the formula is: $13.12 + (0.6215 \cdot T) - (11.37 \cdot V^{0.16}) + (0.3965 \cdot T \cdot V^{0.16})$. Make sure you label your output properly. For example:

```
At temperature 5 degrees C and wind speed 20 km/hr,
the wind chill temperature is 1.0669572525115663.
```

You will need to explicitly bind the values for your temperature and wind speed variables, since we have not discussed how to get user input. That is in Chapter 4, Interacting with Web Pages, on page 47. You can see a solution at code/first-project/src/WindChill.re.

Summing Up

Congratulations! You now know how to write, compile, and run simple ReasonML programs. You've learned how to work with numbers, perform conditional operations, and output strings. You've also seen how ReasonML's type system keeps you from accidentally mixing types.

In the next chapter, we will look at one of the most important concepts in ReasonML: functions.

CHAPTER 2

Writing Functions

ReasonML is a functional programming language, which allows you to take advantage of the many benefits of that programming style. Pure functions (functions that have no side effects) make debugging and testing easier. You never have to worry about your function changing some global state, which, in turn, makes things like concurrent and asynchronous code much easier to write.

This chapter is concerned mostly with the mechanics of writing functions. We'll look at syntax shortcuts and labeled parameters that let you specify arguments by name rather than order. We'll also discuss how ReasonML's type inference automatically checks that our functions' parameters and results have the right types. Though, as you'll see, function annotations let you explicitly describe the types required for parameters and return values.

ReasonML's functions share the same purpose as functions in other languages —allowing you to write more modular, reusable code. As in JavaScript, functions in ReasonML are *first class*. You can pass a function as an argument to another function, and you can write a function that returns a new function as its result. This last ability produces the superpower of currying, which lets you create a new function by applying only some of a function's arguments. Together, first-class functions and currying let you write much more flexible code.

Defining Functions

Let's jump right in and define a function that takes the average of two floating-point numbers and binds that function to the symbol avg:

functions/src/Functions.re
```
let avg = (a, b) => {
  (a +. b) /. 2.0;
};
```

A function definition begins with the parameters in parentheses, followed by a thick arrow =>, then the body of the function enclosed in braces. The last expression in the braces (in this case, the only expression) is the function's return value.

Once you have avg() defined, you can call the function in your code. In fact, ReasonML *requires* you to define your functions before you use them:

functions/src/Functions.re
```
let result = avg(3.0, 4.5);
Js.log(result);
```

And here it is in action:

```
code/functions> bsb -make-world
ninja: Entering directory `lib/bs'
[3/3] Building src/Functions.mlast.d
[1/1] Building src/Functions-Simplefunctions.cmj
code/functions> node src/Functions.bs.js
3.75
```

Let's write a more complex function to find the monthly payment on a loan using this formula:

$$payment = p \cdot \frac{r(1+r)^n}{(1+r)^n - 1}$$

Where p is the principal, r is the monthly interest rate, and n is the number of months of the loan. Ordinarily, you'd see the interest rate of a loan quoted as an annual percentage rate (APR) and a number of years. So our function will have to do a bit of work:

functions/src/Functions.re
```
let payment = (principal, apr, years) => {
  let r = (apr /. 12.0) /. 100.0;
  let n = float_of_int(years * 12);
  let powerTerm = (1.0 +. r) ** n;
  principal *. (r *. powerTerm) /. (powerTerm -. 1.0);
};

let amount = payment(10000.0, 5.0, 30);
Js.log2("Amount per month: $", amount);
```

Let's go through this function line by line. The first line binds the variable payment to a function with three parameters: principal, apr, and years.

The next three lines bind local variables. The rate r is a monthly rate as a decimal, so we need to divide the annual percentage rate by 12 to convert years to months, and by 100 to convert from percent to decimal.

Since payments are monthly, n is bound to years * 12. n is used with the ** operator, which requires floats. That's why we used float_of_int().

The last variable, powerTerm, is just for convenience, so we do not have to write (1.0 +. r) ** n twice when evaluating the result, which is in the last line of the function. The last expression evaluated in a function is its return value, so there's no need to bind it to a variable and use a return statement as you might need in other programming languages.

Compiling and running gives us this output (with the output of the compiler and the result of the avg() call omitted):

```
code/functions> node src/Functions.bs.js
Amount per month: $ 53.68216230121382
```

That output leaves something to be desired—we really want to display two decimal places. We'll use JavaScript's toFixedWithPrecision() method from the Js.Float module.

functions/src/Functions.re
```
Js.log2("Amount per month: $",
        Js.Float.toFixedWithPrecision(amount, ~digits=2));
```

Here's what the output looks like when we run it again (showing only the new output):

```
code/functions> node src/Functions.bs.js
Amount per month: $ 53.68
```

There's something new in the call: ~digits=2. This is a *labeled parameter*, so let's address that topic right now.

Using Labeled Parameters

The authors of toFixedWithPrecision() wanted you to be able to use that function without ever having to remember whether the number of digits was the first or the last parameter. Similarly, there is nothing wrong with the payment() function, but it would be nice if people using it did not have to remember the order of the parameters. ReasonML lets you label parameters by preceding the parameter names with the ~ character. Here's the payment() function with labeled parameters:

functions/src/LabeledParams.re

```
let payment = (~principal, ~apr, ~years) => {
  let r = apr /. 12.0 /. 100.0;
  let n = float_of_int(years * 12);
  let powerTerm = (1.0 +. r) ** n;
  principal *. (r *. powerTerm) /. (powerTerm -. 1.0);
};
```

While you can still call the function without using the labels:

```
let amount = payment(10000.0, 5.0, 30);
```

The compiler will give you a warning:

```
code/functions/src/LabeledParams.re 11:14-20

10
11  |  let amount = payment(10000.0, 5.0, 30);
12

labels were omitted in the application of this function.
```

To avoid the warning, you label the arguments, which you can then specify in any order:

functions/src/LabeledParams.re

```
let amount = payment(~principal=10000.0, ~apr=5.0, ~years=30);
Js.log2("Amount per month for loan 1: $",
        Js_float.toFixedWithPrecision(amount, ~digits=2));

let amount2 = payment(~apr=7.5, ~years=15, ~principal=25000.0);
Js.log2("Amount per month for loan 2: $",
        Js_float.toFixedWithPrecision(amount2, ~digits=2));
```

```
code/functions> node src/LabeledParams.bs.js
Amount per month for loan 1: $ 53.68
Amount per month for loan 2: $ 231.75
```

Labeled parameters can also have aliases. If, for example, you're a purist and want to use the name p in the last step of the formula while still providing the name principal to your users, you could rewrite the function like this:

```
➤    let payment = (~principal as p, ~apr, ~years) => {
     let r = apr /. 12.0 /. 100.0;
     let n = float_of_int(years * 12);
     let powerTerm = (1.0 +. r) ** n;
➤    p *. (r *. powerTerm) /. (powerTerm -. 1.0); /* using p here */
   };
```

> **Behind the Scenes**
>
> In fact, what we did in the first line is un-sugaring! This code:
>
> ```
> let payment = (~principal, ~apr, ~years)
> ```
>
> is syntactic sugar for the following—and aren't you glad you don't have to type it out every time you use labeled parameters?
>
> ```
> let payment = (~principal as principal, ~apr as apr,
>     ~years as years)
> ```

Providing Default Values for Labeled Parameters

In the United States, the standard for mortgages is a 30-year loan. If the majority of our users are in the US, we might want to provide a default of 30 for years. In order to provide default values, we need to have at least one unlabeled parameter because of the way ReasonML does currying, as described on page 27. All our parameters are labeled, so we'll add a special parameter () called *unit* as an unlabeled, do-nothing parameter:

functions/src/DefaultParams.re
```
let payment = (~principal, ~apr, ~years=30, ()) => {
  let r = apr /. 12.0 /. 100.0;
  let n = float_of_int(years * 12);
  let powerTerm = (1.0 +. r) ** n;
  principal *. (r *. powerTerm) /. (powerTerm -. 1.0);
};
```

When you call the function, you must provide unit, written as (), as one of the parameters:

functions/src/DefaultParams.re
```
let amount = payment(~principal=10000.0, ~apr=5.0, ());
Js.log2("Amount per month for loan 1: $",
        Js.Float.toFixedWithPrecision(amount, ~digits=2));

let amount2 = payment(~apr=7.5, ~years=15, ~principal=25000.0, ());
Js.log2("Amount per month for loan 2: $",
        Js.Float.toFixedWithPrecision(amount2, ~digits=2));
```

It's also possible to have optional parameters, but we can't discuss that until we go over variant types on page 30.

Shortening Code with refmt

All the functions we've written so far have been fully written out. Here, for example, is a function that squares its argument:

```
let sqr = (x) => {
  x * x;
};
```

This function doesn't take advantage of any of ReasonML's syntactic sugar. Syntactic sugar is syntax that makes programs easier to read or write, thus making your life sweeter. If a function has only one parameter, you don't need to enclose it in parentheses. If there's only one expression in the body of the function, you don't need the braces. You'd write the function in its most compact form this way:

```
let sqr = x => x * x;
```

Perhaps you'd like to keep your code as compact as possible, but you don't want to waste neurons wondering if the rules allow you to leave out punctuation or not. Never fear—when you installed BuckleScript you got the bsrefmt program. It will parse your ReasonML code and apply the syntax sugar for you. In its simplest form, you provide the name of the file, and bsrefmt outputs the reformatted code to standard output (your terminal). Here's an example of running the program and redirecting the output to a file:

```
/code/functions> bsrefmt src/Functions.re > src/ReformattedFunctions.re
```

A comparison of the files shows these before and after changes:

Before:
```
let avg = (a, b) => {
  (a +. b) /. 2.0;
};
```

After:
```
let avg = (a, b) => (a +. b) /. 2.0;
```

Before:
```
Js.log2("Amount per month: $",
        Js.Float.toFixedWithPrecision(amount, ~digits=2));
```

After:
```
Js.log2(
  "Amount per month: $",
  Js.Float.toFixedWithPrecision(amount, ~digits=2),
);
```

Some ReasonML editor plugins let you set an option to automatically reformat code every time you save your file, so there's no need to manually run bsrefmt.

Here's some bonus syntactic sugar for you: *punning.* If you are calling a function with labeled parameters and you are passing a variable with the same name as the parameter, you don't have to repeat the variable name. In the following code, the last two lines are equivalent:

functions/src/DefaultParams.re
```
let apr = 7.5;
let principal = 10000.0;
let month1 = payment(~principal=principal, ~apr=apr, ~years=15, ());
let month2 = payment(~principal, ~apr, ~years=15, ());
```

Shortening Function Names

If you're tired of typing a long name like Js.Float.toFixedWithPrecision, you can bind that name to a shorter name and use that instead:

```
let toFixed = Js.Float.toFixedWithPrecision;
let example = toFixed(3.1415926, ~digits=4);
```

We're binding one symbol to another. We don't put any parentheses after the function name on the right-hand side—that would be a function call, and that's not what we want.

Specifying Parameter Types

In the introduction on page 5, we mentioned that ReasonML's static type system keeps you from making the sort of errors that can sink a dynamically typed program. You might be feeling a bit cheated in that we haven't done a single bit of type specification so far in this chapter. That's because ReasonML's type inference engine has been doing a fantastic job of figuring everything out for us.

If, for example, you try to call the payment() function with an integer for the annual percentage rate, the compiler won't permit it:

```
We've found a bug for you!
code/functions/src/TypeSpecifications.re 25:48

23 |
24 |
25 |   let badCall = payment(~principal=10000.0, ~apr=5, ~years=15);
26 |
27 |

This has type:
  int
But somewhere wanted:
  float
```

You can convert a int to a float with float_of_int.
If this is a literal, you want a number with a
trailing dot (e.g. 20.).

It seems like ReasonML knows the types, but how can we see what it has determined? Many editor plugins for ReasonML will show you the *type signatures* (the types of parameters and the return type), also called *type annotation* for functions:

```
                 (~principal: float, ~apr: float, ~years: int) ⇒ float
17    let payment = (~principal, ~apr, ~years) => {
18      let r = apr /. 12.0 /. 100.0;
19      let n = float_of_int(years * 12);
20      let powerTerm = (1.0 +. r) ** n;
21      principal *. (r *. powerTerm) /. (powerTerm -. 1.0);
22    };
```

Should I Annotate My Functions?

The automatic type inference works so well that many people in the ReasonML community recommend that you not annotate, but instead let the inference engine do its work. I'm going to be the heretic here and suggest there are several reasons for annotating:

First, there are times when the inference engine can't make an unambiguous conclusion, and you *must* tell ReasonML what types are intended. Second, when you write an API or functions for other people to use, you can create an interface file that exposes the functions you want to be exported—the annotations serve as part of the API documentation. Finally, I've found that writing annotations keeps me focused on what input and output the functions expect, and this encourages me to do more pre-planning before I write code.

The good news of annotation is that your functions accept the exact types that you specify. The bad news is that your functions accept the exact types that you specify, and those may be more restrictive than what the type inference engine would have chosen for you.

On all these points, your mileage may vary.

To annotate a function, follow each of the parameters by a colon : and the data type for that parameter. After the closing parenthesis of the parameters, put another colon and the function's return type. As an example, here are the annotations of the functions we've written so far. Notice how we're using unit as the data type for () in the last annotation:

```
functions/src/Annotations.re
let avg = (a: float, b: float) : float => {
let payment = (~principal: float, ~apr: float,
                ~years: int=30, ():unit) : float=> {
```

It's also possible to annotate a function definition in a style that specifies the parameter types first, then the parameters:

```
functions/src/AlternateAnnotation.re
let avg: (float, float) => float =
        (a, b) => {
let payment:
  (~principal: float, ~apr: float, ~years: int=?, unit) => float =
  (~principal, ~apr, ~years = 30, ()) => {
```

If you are coming to ReasonML from Haskell, this alternate form is more familiar to you—Haskell also separates type information from implementation (separation of concerns).[1] If you are coming from the world of TypeScript or Flow, you may prefer the form where parameters and their types are together. For what it's worth, the majority of ReasonML code that I have seen in the wild uses the form with parameter name and type together rather than this alternate form.

Writing Functions without Parameters or Return Values

All the functions we've written so far have been much like the functions you know from math: they take one or more arguments and return some value. (Similarly, our functions always return the same values for the same inputs —they're *pure functions*.)

Some functions don't require any inputs—the Js.Math.random() function doesn't need any input argument. Calling it will give you back a random number from 0.0 to 1.0, and you'll get a different one every time. When calling a function with no parameters, you *must* provide the parentheses after the function name:

```
functions/src/UsingUnit.re
let random1 = Js.Math.random();
Js.log(random1);

let random2 = Js.Math.random;
Js.log(random2);
```

If you run this code, you'll see this output:

```
0.03326409915331441
[Function: random2]
```

The first call does what we expect. The second call—without parentheses— has the effect of binding the function Js.Math.random to the symbol random2, which is probably not what we had in mind.

---

1. en.wikipedia.org/wiki/Separation_of_concerns

Other functions, like Js.log(), don't provide any useful return value. We only love Js.log() for its *side effect* of putting text on the terminal. So how do we write our own functions with no output? The answer is unit.

Here's a function you might write to help provide debug output. This function has input parameters but provides no return value, so its return type is unit, which is what Js.log() returns.

functions/src/UsingUnit.re
```
let debugInt = (varName: string, value: int) : unit => {
  Js.log(varName ++ " is: " ++ string_of_int(value));
};
```

Here's a function that outputs a separator line, so you can visually divide your output into sections. This function has neither input parameters nor a return value:

functions/src/UsingUnit.re
```
let separator = () : unit => {
  Js.log("---------------");
};
```

If you want to explicitly return a unit value, use a pair of parentheses, as in the following function—intended as a good example of an example rather than as useful code:

functions/src/UsingUnit.re
```
let doNothing = (): unit => {
  ();
};
```

Currying: Handling One Argument at a Time

What would happen if we called the avg() function but only gave it one argument? Surely we'd get some sort of error:

functions/src/Currying.re
```
let avg = (a: float, b: float) : float => {
  (a +. b) /. 2.0;
};

Js.log2("Average of 3 and 4", avg(3.0, 4.0));
Js.log2("Average of 3?!", avg(3.0));
```

```
code/functions> bsb -make-world
ninja: Entering directory `lib/bs'
[3/3] Building src/Currying.mlast.d
[1/1] Building src/Currying-Simplefunctions.cmj
code/functions> node src/Currying.bs.js
Average of 3 and 4 3.5
```

```
Average of 3?! function (param) {
    return avg(3.0, param);
}
```

It compiles without errors, and when we run it, we get a function as output rather than an error message. What strange sorcery is this? It's *currying*, a term named after the mathematician and logician Haskell Curry. To understand what currying is, imagine a cell phone's contact list. A phone number consists of a country code, an area code, and a number. Look at this phone contact list:

The entry for Kim has a full phone number with country 49, area code 030, and phone number 118 99. The other entries are partial entries—for example, the entry for Germany shows only its country code, and Berlin shows only the country and area code. If you were to select the entry for Berlin on a regular cell phone, it would dial 49 030, which is an invalid number. But this imaginary cell phone is magic—when you select Berlin:

The phone presents you with those digits and waits for you to enter the rest of the phone number. This would save a lot of time if you have to call many people in Berlin who aren't in the contact list. You could bring up Berlin in the contact list and have much of the number pre-entered.

Rather than attempting to dial a bad number, the magic phone presents a partially complete screen for entering the number if we don't give it all the parts. In a similar way, if we call a ReasonML function with fewer parameters than it expects, ReasonML doesn't try to call the function. Instead, it curries —it gives us back a *new* function with those arguments filled in and space for the remaining parameters.

With that in mind, let's write a function that calls a number when it's given a country code, area, and phone number, and give Kim a call:

functions/src/Currying.re
```
let call = (country: string, area: string, number: string)
  : string => {
    country ++ " " ++ area ++ " " ++ number;
};

Js.log2("Call Kim at", call("49", "030", "118 99"));
```

```
/code/functions> node src/Currying.bs.js
Call Kim at 49 030 118 99
```

Now we'll create a function for dialing people in Germany, and another one for dialing Berlin:

functions/src/Currying.re
```
let callGermany = call("049");
let callBerlin = call("049", "030");

Js.log2("Call Germany:", callGermany);
Js.log2("Call Berlin:", callBerlin);
```

```
/code/functions> node src/Currying.bs.js
Call Germany: function callGermany(param, param$1) {
  return call("049", param, param$1);
}
Call Berlin: function callBerlin(param) {
  return call("049", "030", param);
}
```

When calling these new functions, we need to provide only the missing parameters:

```
functions/src/Currying.re
Js.log2("Call someone in Germany:", callGermany("040", "118 01"));
Js.log2("Call someone in Berlin:", callBerlin("118 23"));
```

```
code/functions> node src/Currying.bs.js
Call someone in Germany: 049 040 118 01
Call someone in Berlin: 049 030 118 23
```

You can even use curried functions as the basis of other curried functions. We could also have written:

```
let callGermany = call("049");    /* same as before */
let callBerlin = callGermany("030"); /* uses curried callGermany() */
```

In summary: currying lets you call a function with fewer parameters than specified in the function definition. Instead of giving you an error, ReasonML gives you a new function with your parameters filled in.

Currying and Default Values

In the case of default parameters on page 19, we needed to provide unit as an unlabeled parameter. Otherwise, this code would be ambiguous:

```
let amount = payment(~principal=10000.0, ~apr=5.0);
```

Is this a call to payment() with all its parameters (using the default value for ~years), or is it a call to payment() that's really curried and awaiting that last parameter? ReasonML solves this dilemma by saying, "If there is a positional (non-labeled) argument, then this is a complete call with a default value. Otherwise, it's curried." And that's why we need to make our intention clear by putting in the unit. (In this case, we use unit because we have no unlabeled parameters.) For all the details on currying, see the ReasonML documentation at reasonml.github.io/docs/en/function.html#currying.

Currying and Labeled Parameters

As an alternative to default values, you can use currying with labeled parameters. In the example code we wrote on page 19, the default was appropriate for US mortgages. Rather than have one function with a single default, currying lets you create *several* functions with different values for one or more of the parameters. In this code, we create payment calculation functions for standard mortgage lengths in the US (30 years), UK (25 years), and Germany (20 years):

```
functions/src/CurryingWithNames.re
let usPayment = payment(~years=30);
let ukPayment = payment(~years=25);
let dePayment = payment(~years=20);

let toFixed = Js.Float.toFixedWithPrecision;

Js.log("Loan of 10000 at 5%");
Js.log2({js|US: $|js},
        toFixed(usPayment(~principal=10000.0, ~apr=5.0), ~digits=2));
Js.log2({js|UK: £|js},
        toFixed(ukPayment(~principal=10000.0, ~apr=5.0), ~digits=2));
Js.log2({js|DE: €|js},
        toFixed(dePayment(~principal=10000.0, ~apr=5.0), ~digits=2));
```

```
code/functions> node src/CurryingWithNames.bs.js
Loan of 10000 at 5%
US: $ 53.68
UK: £ 58.46
DE: € 66.00
```

It's Your Turn

Write a function named discount() that calculates discount prices. It should have two labeled parameters (choose any names you like):

- The original price, which is float
- The discount percent, which is also float

If the original price is, say, $30.00 and the discount percent is 5%, the amount saved is $1.50 (5% of $30.00), making the result $28.50.

Then, use currying to create functions named halfOff() which uses 50 as the value for the percent, and tenPercentOff(), which uses 10 as the value for the percent. Write complete type annotations on the discount() function. Make sure you write code that uses these functions and displays the results so you can be sure everything works! You can see a solution at code/functions/src/Discount.re.

Summing Up

You can now write functions that have labeled parameters (making them more flexible to call). Reason's automatic type inference gives your functions type safety, but you can now annotate the parameter types manually if you prefer. Finally, you can use currying to make new functions that have some of their arguments already filled in.

So far, the functions we've covered use ReasonML's built-in data types. What if you need to represent other data types? The next chapter will give us the answers to this question.

CHAPTER 3

Creating Your Own Data Types

In this chapter, you will learn how to go beyond ReasonML's built-in data types such as int, float, and string by defining your own data types. This powerful capability will help you build reliable, robust programs. In addition to letting you express your programs in terms that mirror your data structures, data types give you these extra advantages:

- You can create data types such as Price or Discount to ensure type safety—the compiler will make sure you can't ever pass a Discount as an argument to a function that expects a Price.

- You can create *variant data types* that specify a set of valid values. For example, in a survey, you might define a type with values Agree, Disagree, and Neutral. ReasonML's compiler will make sure that those are the *only* possible values a variable of that type can have, and it will not allow nonexistent values like the misspelled Nuetral.

- ReasonML's built-in option type formalizes the representation of values that could be invalid. The compiler makes sure you handle both valid and invalid cases, avoiding null or undefined values. This will be incredibly useful when you interact with web pages, where you might have to handle invalid user-entered data.

In all these cases, ReasonML moves the detection of a large class of errors from runtime to compile time.

Best of all, ReasonML's type inference system automatically recognizes the data types you're using—you don't have to explicitly specify data types everywhere.

Renaming a Data Type

A data type *alias* is the simplest of all custom data types—it gives a new name to an existing data type. For example, if you want types to represent test scores and percents, you could do this:

```
type scoreType = int;
type percentType = float;

let calcPercent = (score: scoreType, max: scoreType) : percentType =>
  float_of_int(score) /. float_of_int(max) *. 100.0;
```

The only advantage of using a data type alias is to increase readability, though you might also achieve this by using labeled parameters. Aliases don't give you any type safety. You can still write meaningless code like this:

datatypes/src/BizarreAliases.re
```
type scoreType = int;
type percentType = float;

type userId = int;

/* Explicitly annotate this type to make a point */
let person: userId = 60;

let calcPercent = (score: scoreType, max: scoreType) : percentType =>
  float_of_int(score) /. float_of_int(max) *. 100.0;

let result = calcPercent(person, 75);
Js.log({j|Bogus result is $result|j}); /* output: Bogus result is 80 */
```

Since the aliases are mere alternate names, the code can merrily pass what is purportedly a userId data type to a parameter expecting a scoreType. This is less than ideal to say the least.

Creating Variant Data Types

Here's where ReasonML's type system begins to show some of its power. Let's say we want a data type to represent shirt sizes: Small, Medium, Large, and XLarge (extra-large). We could use an alias for the string type, but it wouldn't keep us from doing things like this:

datatypes/src/StringSizes.re
```
type shirtSize = string;

let mySize = "Medium";
let otherSize = "Large";
let wrongSize = "M";
```

ReasonML lets us create a data type that allows only valid values with a *data type constructor*, which, as its name implies, tells us how to construct a value of that particular data type. This is called a *variant data type*, as we're specifying the various values the data type can have:

```
type shirtSize =
  | Small
  | Medium
  | Large
  | XLarge;
```

Constructor names *must* begin with a capital letter. We can bind shirtSize values to variables. The first example has its type annotated:

```
let mySize: shirtSize = Medium;
let otherSize = Large;
```

The constructors for a variant data type give you all the possible values. But they're *not* strings! Doing the following:

```
let badSize: shirtSize = "Medium";
```

Gives us this error:

```
We've found a bug for you!
/path/to/code/datatypes/src/ShirtSizes.re 16:26-33

15 |
16 |   let badSize: shirtSize = "Medium";

This has type:
  string
But somewhere wanted:
  shirtSize
```

If we try to create a shirtSize binding with an illegal value:

```
let badSize: shirtSize = M;
```

The compiler tells us that we've used a value that isn't in our data type:

```
We've found a bug for you!
/path/to/code/datatypes/src/ShirtSizes.re 16:26

15 |
16 |   let badSize: shirtSize = M;

This variant expression is expected to have type shirtSize
The constructor M doesn't belong to type shirtSize
```

Using Variant Data Types

Let's say that a small shirt costs $11.00, a medium costs $12.50, a large costs $14.00, and an extra-large costs $16.00. We can write a function to return the price of a shirt given its size:

datatypes/src/ShirtSizes.re
```
let priceIf = (size: shirtSize) : float => {
  if (size === Small) {
    11.00
  } else if (size === Medium) {
    12.50
  } else if (size === Large) {
    14.00
  } else {
    16.00
  }
};

Js.log(priceIf(mySize)); /* output: 12.5 */
Js.log(priceIf(otherSize)); /* output: 14 */
```

But it's much more common in ReasonML to use a switch expression to *pattern match* the size:

datatypes/src/ShirtSizes.re
```
let price = (size: shirtSize) : float => {
  switch (size) {
    | Small => 11.00
    | Medium => 12.50
    | Large => 14.00
    | XLarge => 16.00
  }
};

Js.log(price(mySize)); /* output: 12.5 */
Js.log(price(otherSize)); /* output: 14 */
```

Each of the variants (patterns) is preceded by a vertical bar | and followed by a thick arrow =>, which is followed by the expression to yield for that variant. You can think of the vertical bar as introducing an alternative to match to. ReasonML attempts to match the value size with each of the patterns in the order given. When we do a pattern match on a variant data type, we *must* account for all the variants. If we were to leave off the pattern match for XLarge, we would get this error:

```
Warning number 8
28 |
29 |   let price = (size: shirtSize) : float => {
30 |     switch (size) {
 . |     ...
34 |     }
35 |   };
36 |
```

You forgot to handle a possible value here, for example:
XLarge

Let's use switch to write a function that converts a shirtSize value to a string giving the abbreviation for the sizes:

```
let stringOfShirtSize = (size: shirtSize) : string => {
  switch (size) {
    | Small => "S"
    | Medium => "M"
    | Large => "L"
    | XLarge => "XL"
  };
};

Js.log(stringOfShirtSize(mySize)); /* output: M */
```

We absolutely need the stringOfShirtSize() function. Consider this code:

```
type shirtSize =
  | Small
  | Medium
  | Large
  | XLarge;

let mySize = Medium;
Js.log2("Size is", mySize);
```

Here's what you get when you run it:

```
you@computer:~/book_projects/datatypes> node src/PrintType.bs.js
Size is 1
```

What's going on here?! Why do we get a number? The answer is that all of ReasonML's type checking and manipulation is done entirely at compile time. Once the types are checked, ReasonML is free to use any internal form it likes to represent the types. In this case, it is optimized into numeric form at run-time, as we can see in the JavaScript code that was generated:

datatypes/src/PrintType.bs.js
```
// Generated by BUCKLESCRIPT VERSION 5.0.0-dev.4, PLEASE EDIT WITH CARE
'use strict';

console.log("Size is", /* Medium */1);

var mySize = /* Medium */1;

exports.mySize = mySize;
/*  Not a pure module */
```

The moral of the story: ReasonML's data types exist only at compile time. If you want to display the value in a readable form, you must provide a function to convert the type to a string.

We'll also want a function that converts a string parameter, an abbreviation for the size, to a shirtSize value. But we have a problem: what happens if someone gives us a bad string, such as "N" or "Medium"? If switch requires us to write out all possible values, how do we handle all possible strings? Luckily, switch is provided with a catch-all pattern, _ (underscore), which stands for "any case that hasn't been matched yet."

datatypes/src/ShirtSizes.re
```
let shirtSizeOfString = (str: string) : shirtSize => {
  switch (str) {
    | "S" => Small
    | "M" => Medium
    | "L" => Large
    | "XL" => XLarge
    | _ => Medium
  }
};
```

Our approach in this code is to throw our hands up in the air and say, "If we can't figure out what you want, we'll give you Medium." If you aren't thrilled with this, don't worry—we'll find a better way to handle this later in the chapter.

Creating Variant Data Types with Parameters

Shirt sizes don't end with extra-large. There are double, triple, and even quadruple extra-large, usually abbreviated as XXL, XXXL, and XXXXL. Parameterized types let us specify a parameter for the constructor. In our case, we want the parameter to tell us how many Xs are on the shirt size.

Here's a parameterized version of the shirt size constructor (it has the same name, but it's in a separate file):

datatypes/src/ParamShirtSizes.re
```
type shirtSize =
  | Small
  | Medium
  | Large
  | XLarge(int);
```

The last line says that to construct an XLarge variant, you need to provide an integer, which we'll use to tell how many "extras" we want:

datatypes/src/ParamShirtSizes.re
```
let mySize: shirtSize = Medium;
let bigSize = XLarge(1);
let veryBigSize = XLarge(3);
```

When it comes to setting the price, let's say that XLarge(1) costs $16.00, plus $0.50 for every additional X. We modify the switch to accept the parameter and use it:

datatypes/src/ParamShirtSizes.re
```
Line 1  let price = (size: shirtSize) : float => {
   -      switch (size) {
   -        | Small => 11.00
   -        | Medium => 12.50
   5        | Large => 14.00
   -        | XLarge(n) => 16.00 +.
   -            (float_of_int(n - 1) *. 0.50)
   -      }
   -    };
  10
   -  Js.log(price(mySize)); /* output: 12.5 */
   -  Js.log(price(bigSize)); /* output: 16 */
   -  Js.log(price(veryBigSize)); /* output: 17 */
```

Line 6 uses *destructuring* to extract the parameter from the size variable. For example, if size were XLarge(3), n would have the value 3 in the calculation. In addition to extracting parameters, destructuring also lets you extract fields from a data structure. We'll see this come into play in later chapters.

The next function to modify is stringOfShirtSize(). Again, we need destructuring to extract the parameter n in variants of the form XLarge(n) and make a string of that many Xs. The make() function in BuckleScript's String module[1] does exactly that.

---

1. reasonml.github.io/api/String.html

datatypes/src/ParamShirtSizes.re
```
let stringOfShirtSize = (size: shirtSize) : string => {
  switch (size) {
    | Small => "S"
    | Medium => "M"
    | Large => "L"
    | XLarge(n) => String.make(n, 'X') ++ "L"
  };
};

Js.log(stringOfShirtSize(veryBigSize)); /* output: XXXL */
```

Note that the second argument to make() is a character in single quotes. We'll solve the problem of repeating a multi-character string when we discuss recursion on on page 94.

The shirtSizeOfString() function needs the addition of a few lines to handle the new "extra" sizes (showing only the additions here):

datatypes/src/ParamShirtSizes.re
```
| "L" => Large
| "XL" => XLarge(1)
| "XXL" => XLarge(2)
| "XXXL" => XLarge(3)
| "XXXXL" => XLarge(4)
| _ => Medium
```

This function still leaves the issue of what to do with invalid strings—it's still blindly assigning Medium. Let's find a better way to handle this after you first try your hand at creating a variant data type.

It's Your Turn

Create a variant data type called colorSpec that lets you specify a color in one of these ways:

```
let color1 = White;
let color2 = Black;
let color3 = Gray(0.50); /* Percentage gray as a float */
let color4 = RGB(255, 255, 255); /* Integers for Red, Green, and Blue */
```

Write a function that converts a colorSpec to a string in the form rgb(r,g,b). Here's the starting point for your function:

```
let stringOfColorSpec = (cspec: colorSpec) : string => {
  /* your code here */
};
```

Here are examples of what it produces:

> ## Using One-Variant Data Types
>
> Now that we know how to create a variant data type with a parameter, we can improve on the bogus example that we made with aliases on page 30.
>
> Instead of aliases, we define the score, percent, and user ID types as data type constructors:
>
> datatypes/src/SingleVariant.re
> ```
> type scoreType = Score(int);
> type percentType = Percent(float);
> type userId = UserId(int);
> ```
>
> When we use variables of these parameterized types, we must construct values, as in line 1, and destructure them, as in line 4.
>
> datatypes/src/SingleVariant.re
> ```
> Line 1  let person: userId = UserId(60);
>
>         let calcPercent = (score: scoreType, max: scoreType) : percentType => {
>           let Score(s) = score;
>      5    let Score(m) = max;
>           Percent(float_of_int(s) /. float_of_int(m) *. 100.0);
>         };
>
>         /* Won't compile. Comment out next line to get a working program */
>     10  /*let result = calcPercent(person, Score(75));*//**/
>
>         let Percent(result) = calcPercent(Score(40), Score(75));
>         Js.log({j|Good result is $result|j}); /* output: Good result is 53.33333... */
> ```
>
> Using these data types gives us type safety. ReasonML will complain in line 10 that you're trying to use a userId where a score is required.

```
Js.log(stringOfColorSpec(White)); /* rgb(255,255,255) */
Js.log(stringOfColorSpec(Black)); /* rgb(0,0,0) */
Js.log(stringOfColorSpec(Gray(0.5))); /* rgb(127,127,127) */
Js.log(stringOfColorSpec(RGB(64, 128, 192))); /* rgb(64,128,192) */
```

Writing a colorSpecOfString() is tricky because you need to handle a much larger range of possible inputs than you'd need for the shirt sizes, so let's not go for that one right now. You can see a solution in file code/datatypes/src/ColorSpec.re.

Using the option Type

In JavaScript, we could have solved the problem of bad input for shirtSizeOfString() by returning null or undefined, but that leads to all manner of difficulties. What we really want is a way to handle invalid data in a type-safe manner.

ReasonML solves the problem with a built-in variant data type named option. If you were to write it yourself, it would look like this:

```
type option('a) =
  | Some('a)
  | None;
```

This is a *parametric data type* (see What's a Parametric Data Type?, on page 38 for details) where 'a is a *type variable*. The leading single quote is required for type variables.

\\// Joe asks:
ʒʃ What's a Parametric Data Type?

Functions use parameters as placeholders that get filled in by argument values. In a similar way, instead of having to write specialized option types for each possible basic data type:

```
type optionInt =
  | Some(int)
  | None;
type optionFloat =
  | Some(float)
  | None;
let x: optionInt = Some(3);
let y: optionFloat = Some(4.0);
```

We can write the following definition using the *type parameter* 'a:

```
type option('a) =
  | Some('a)
  | None;
```

Type parameter names must begin with a single quote. Unlike function parameters, which are filled in by a number or string value, the type parameter 'a is filled in by a *data type*. Now, rather than writing multiple specialized types, we can define a single parametric data type and "fill in the blank" with any data type we need:

```
let x: option(int) = Some(3);
let y: option(float) = Some(4.0);
let z: option(shirtSize) = Some(XL);
```

Parametric data types are similar to what other languages call *generics*.

The Some('a) variant indicates valid data; None represents what would normally be null or undefined in other languages. Using the option data type doesn't mean we can never have invalid data. Rather, option gives us an organized way of dealing with invalid data within ReasonML's type system.

Instead of accepting that an invalid string passed to shirtSizeOfString() returns Medium as the default, we rewrite the function to return an option(shirtSize):

```
datatypes/src/OptionShirtSizes.re
let shirtSizeOfString = (str: string) : option(shirtSize) => {
  switch (str) {
    | "S" => Some(Small)
    | "M" => Some(Medium)
    | "L" => Some(Large)
    | "XL" => Some(XLarge(1))
    | "XXL" => Some(XLarge(2))
    | "XXXL" => Some(XLarge(3))
    | "XXXXL" => Some(XLarge(4))
    | _ => None
  }
};
```

For valid strings, the function returns a shirtSize wrapped in Some(). Invalid strings return None. We can rewrite the price() function to accept an option(shirtSize) and return an option(float):

```
datatypes/src/OptionShirtSizes.re
let price = (size: option(shirtSize)) : option(float) => {
  switch (size) {
    | Some(Small) => Some(11.00)
    | Some(Medium) => Some(12.50)
    | Some(Large) => Some(14.00)
    | Some(XLarge(n)) => Some(16.00 +. (float_of_int(n - 1) *. 0.50))
    | None => None
  }
};
```

Once we're in option-land, we *must* account for both the Some() and None cases. At some point, we have to unwrap the value from the Some() or handle None when we need to give a final result.

```
datatypes/src/OptionShirtSizes.re
let toFixed = Js.Float.toFixedWithPrecision;

let displayPrice = (input: string) : unit => {
  let size = shirtSizeOfString(input);
  let amount = price(size);
  let text = switch (amount) {
    | Some(cost) => {
        let costStr = toFixed(cost, ~digits=2);
        {j|Your $input shirt costs \$$costStr.|j}
      }

    | None => {j|Cannot determine price for $input|j}
  };
  Js.log(text);
};

displayPrice("XXL"); /* output: Your XXL shirt costs $16.50. */
```

Because the $ interpolates variables inside {j|...|j}, if we want a true dollar sign, we must escape it with a backslash as \$.

Working with option Values

In a program of any significant length, we'll eventually end up passing option values through a series of functions, some of which accept and/or return option values, and some that don't. Consider these functions:

```
datatypes/src/BeltExamples.re
let toFloat = (str: string) : option(float) => {
  let result =  (Js.Float.fromString(str));
  if (Js.Float.isNaN(result)) {
    None
  } else {
    Some(result)
  }
};

let cube = (x: float) : float =>  x *. x *. x;

let reciprocal = (x: float) : option(float) => {
  if (x !== 0.0) {
    Some(1.0 /. x)
  } else {
    None
  }
};
```

We'd like to stitch these together into a program that performs the following steps:

1. Use toFloat() to convert a string to float. Since the string might not be valid, the output has to be option(float).

2. Use reciprocal() to take the reciprocal of the result of step 1. Since we might have been given an invalid value of 0, the output of this function must also be option(float).

3. Use cube() to cube the result of step 2.

4. Convert the result to a string with the help of Js.Float.toFixedWithPrecision().

5. Display the result of step 4, which may be an error message if either step 1 or step 2 failed.

We can do it this way:

```
Line 1   let method1 = (input: string): unit => {
           let x = toFloat(input);
           let oneOver = switch (x) {
             | Some(value) => reciprocal(value)
      5      | None => None
           };
           let result = switch(oneOver) {
             | Some(value) => Some(cube(value))
             | None => None
     10    };
           let output = switch(result) {
             | Some(value) => Some(Js.Float.toFixedWithPrecision(value, ~digits=3))
             | None => None
           };
     15    let resultText = switch (output) {
             | Some(value) => "The result is " ++ value
             | None => "Could not calculate result."
           };
           Js.log(resultText);
     20  };

     method1("2.0"); /* output: The result is 0.125 */
```

In line 4, we need to extract the value of the option that toFloat() returned, because reciprocal() requires a plain value, not an option. The result of reciprocal() is an option.

Line 8 again extracts the value of an option value. If we want to stay in option-land, we need to put the normal return value from cube() into Some().

Similarly, in line 12, we extract a normal value from the option and re-wrap the result in Some().

The switch starting at line 15 takes us out of option-land so we can display an ordinary string.

In all this code, a value of None is passed on from one step to the next. Once you have invalid data, it stays invalid—we can't accidentally use it in a calculation.

Working with Belt.Option

There's nothing wrong with the preceding example—it works as advertised and accounts for possible invalid data. But all of those switches make the code harder to read. The Belt.Option module gives us functions that let us write this sort of code without all the busy work. The Belt.Option module is part of Belt[2] standard library shipped with BuckleScript.

In line 4, we want the value of an option to go to a function that takes an ordinary value and returns an option. In this case, we use the Belt.Option.flatMap() function. This function expects two parameters: an option(..) value, and the name of a function that takes a normal value and returns an option(...).

Belt.Option.flatMap() extracts the value of the option(...) value and passes it to the function you specified. The result is that function's option(...) value:

```
let oneOver = Belt.Option.flatMap(x, reciprocal);
```

Higher Order Functions

Belt.Option.flatMap() is our first encounter with a *higher-order function*, a function that takes a function as one of its parameters. In ReasonML, functions are just another thing that you can bind to a symbol, and you can pass them to functions and return them from functions—just as you would with any other ReasonML value or variable. We'll be using higher-order functions a *lot* in Chapter 5, Using Collections, on page 61.

We're still in option-land—oneOver contains Some(0.5). In line 8 we're passing that option parameter to cube(). We can't use Belt.Option.flatMap() here, because cube() returns a normal value, not an option(...) value.

Instead, we use Belt.Option.map(), which takes an option value and a function with non-option input and output values (like cube()) as its parameters. Belt.Option.map() extracts the value of the option(...) value and passes it to the function you specified. The result is wrapped up into an option(...) as a Some(...) value:

```
let result = Belt.Option.map(oneOver, cube);
```

The variable result now contains Some(0.125).

What if either x or oneOver had come out to None, which would happen if we had done either of these:

```
method1("two"); /* toFloat() returns None */
method1("0.0"); /* reciprocal returns None */
```

When Belt.Option.flatMap() and Belt.Option.map() get None as their first parameter, they return None immediately without ever calling the function you gave them.

---

2. bucklescript.github.io/bucklescript/api/Belt.html

We'd like to use Belt.Option.map() to eliminate the switch before the function call in line 12. toFixedWithPrecision() is another function that takes and returns ordinary values, but it has *two* parameters, not one. No problem. We can call Js.Float.toFixedWithPrecision() with just one of the arguments—the desired number of decimal points. This returns a new function that needs only one argument, namely, the number to be formatted.

```
let output = Belt.Option.map(result,
  Js.Float.toFixedWithPrecision(~digits=3));
```

Currying vs. Partial Application

Technically, currying is "the technique of translating the evaluation of a function that takes multiple arguments into evaluating a sequence of functions, each with a single argument."[3] In ReasonML, all functions are curried, but ReasonML performs optimization so it does not have to create a lot of intermediate functions.[4]

In this expression: Js.Float.toFixedWithPrecision(~digits=3), we did what is usually called *partial application.* This is the process of providing a number of arguments to a function, producing another function with a smaller number of parameters.

Currying and partial application are not the same thing, but they are closely related, and people often use the terms interchangeably.

Here's the rewritten code:

datatypes/src/BeltExamples.re
```
let method2 = (input: string): unit => {
  let x = toFloat(input);
  let oneOver = Belt.Option.flatMap(x, reciprocal);
  let result = Belt.Option.map(oneOver, cube);
  let output = Belt.Option.map(result,
    Js.Float.toFixedWithPrecision(~digits=3));
  let resultText = switch (output) {
    | Some(value) => "The result is " ++ value
    | None => "Could not calculate result."
  };
  Js.log(resultText);
};

method2("2.0"); /* output: The result is 0.125 */
```

---

3.   en.wikipedia.org/wiki/Currying
4.   reasonml.github.io/docs/en/function#currying

Using Pipe First

The preceding code works fine, but it's a bit clunky. Each stage of the calculation is stored in a new variable binding that is used in the next stage. Wouldn't it be nice if we could pass the result of each calculation to the next one without all those variables? We can do exactly that with ->, the *pipe first* operator.

Pipe first says: "take the value to the left of the -> and pipe it to the function on the right." (In older code, you may see |. used as the pipe first operator. You may also see it referred to by its former name: *fast pipe*.)

We'll put the final switch into a function, allowing us to do this:

```
datatypes/src/BeltExamples.re
let makeDisplayText = (s: option(string)): string => {
  switch (s) {
    | Some(value) => "The result is " ++ value
    | None => "Could not calculate result."
  }
};

let method3 = (input: string): unit => {
  toFloat(input)
  -> Belt.Option.flatMap(_, reciprocal)
  -> Belt.Option.map(_, cube)
  -> Belt.Option.map(_, Js.Float.toFixedWithPrecision(~digits=3))
  -> makeDisplayText(_)
  -> Js.log(_)
};

method3("2.0"); /* output: The result is 0.125 */
```

Pipe first places the piped value in the position where the underscore is. The default position is the first parameter (hence the name). When using the default, if the function you're piping to has only one parameter, you don't need to provide parentheses. Using these defaults, we can write an even more compact form:

```
datatypes/src/BeltExamples.re
let method4 = (input: string): unit => {
  toFloat(input)
  -> Belt.Option.flatMap(reciprocal)
  -> Belt.Option.map(cube)
  -> Belt.Option.map(Js.Float.toFixedWithPrecision(~digits=3))
  -> makeDisplayText
  -> Js.log
};
```

In this book, we will use the underscore to make the position of the piped argument explicit—we don't want to sacrifice clarity for compactness.

Pipe First and Pipe Last

If you read older ReasonML code, you might encounter the |>, or *pipe last* operator. Pipe last will pipe the argument on its left to the *last* argument of the function on the right. This operator works nicely with functions whose last argument carries the result, as is common in the Belt modules. Here are some examples comparing pipe first and pipe last:

datatypes/src/PipeExamples.re
```
let f = (a: int, b: int): int => {
  3 * a + b
};

Js.log(5 -> f(7));     /* f(5, 7); result is 22 */
Js.log(5 -> f(7, _)); /* f(7, 5); result is 26 */
Js.log(5 |> f(7));     /* f(7, 5); result is 26 */
```

You can use pipe last here, but best practice is to use pipe first with an underscore placeholder in case you need to pipe to a position other than first.

It's Your Turn

Back in the code on page 38, we had to rewrite the price() function to accept and return option values.

Change it back to an ordinary function and rewrite the code for displayPrice() (see the code on page 39) using Belt.Option.map() to handle the option manipulation. File code/datatypes/src/OptionShirtSizes2.re contains a solution.

Getting Another Perspective

If you're still a bit uncertain of what Belt.Option.map() and Belt.Option.flatMap() do, here's what they'd look like if we were to implement them ourselves:

datatypes/src/BeltExamples.re
```
let myMap = (optValue: option('a), f: ('a) => 'b) : option('b) => {
  switch (optValue) {
    | Some(value) => Some(f(value))
    | None => None
  }
};
```

```
let myFlatMap = (optValue: option('a), f: ('a) => option('b)) :
 option('b) => {
  switch (optValue) {
    | Some(value) => f(value)
    | None => None
  }
};
```

The annotation f: ('a) => option('b) signifies a function taking a parameter of type 'a and returning a value of type option('b).

Similarly, f: ('a) => 'b signifies a function taking a parameter of type 'a and returning a value of type 'b.

These annotations use two different type parameters because a function being applied with map() or flatMap() might return a different data type than its input. We saw this in the code on page 43, where we used map() with Js.Float.toFixedWith-Precision(), which takes a float as input and produces a string as output.

Summing Up

You now know how to create your own variant data types. You can also use option values to work with data that may be invalid without having having null or undefined complicate your life.

We can write a lot of interesting programs at this point, but we have no way of getting user input. That's the topic for our next chapter, where you'll find out how to interact with web pages.

CHAPTER 4

Interacting with Web Pages

Interacting with web pages is a key requirement of web development. In this chapter, we'll move beyond writing output to the terminal window and examine how ReasonML lets you get input from and display output to a web page as part of building web applications.

This means that things are going to get messy, and we're going to have to handle a non-ideal world. We might attempt to access an element that isn't in the HTML page. A user-entered string that should convert to an integer might not—if two is entered instead of 2, for example. In each of these cases, we get an option value as we discussed on page 37. This is where we'll put the Belt.Option library that we saw on page 41 to work to handle a chain of operations, all yielding option values—any of which can potentially fail. (Belt.Option won't prevent the failures, but it will let us process them in a consistent manner.) Finally, we'll have to update the contents of HTML elements to display results. Let's put on our work gloves and get started.

Creating an Example Web Page

We'll be using some of the code we developed in Chapter 3, Creating Your Own Data Types, on page 29 to create a web page that asks for a quantity of shirts and a shirt size. When you click the Calculate button, it'll display the total price. This is what the page looks like:

And here's the HTML, which we've put in the src directory of our project. Each field we're interested in has its own id= attribute:

```
webpage/shirts/src/index.html
<!DOCTYPE html>
<html>
<head>
  <title>Shirts On Line</title>
  <meta http-equiv="Content-Type" content="text/html; charset=utf-8" />
</head>

<body>
  <h1>Shirts On Line</h1>

  <p>
  Quantity: <input type="text" size="3" id="quantity"/>

  Size: <select id="size">
    <option value="S">Small</option>
    <option value="M">Medium</option>
    <option value="L">Large</option>
    <option value="XL">Extra Large</option>
    <option value="XXL">Extra Extra Large</option>
    <option value="XXXL">Triple Extra Large</option>
  </select>

  <button id="calculate">Calculate</button>
  </p>

  <p>
  Your price: $<span id="price"></span>
  </p>

  <script type="text/javascript" src="WebShirts.bs.js"></script>
</body>
</html>
```

Setting Up the Project

We start the project as we have all the projects so far:

```
bsb -init shirts -theme basic-reason
```

Rather than using ReasonML's built-in functions exclusively to create a program we can run via npm, we'll be accessing a web page via the DOM. While ReasonML does provide a limited DOM library via BuckleScript (bucklescript.github.io/bucklescript/api/Dom.html), a more powerful external library is available—bs-webapi (github.com/reasonml-community/bs-webapi-incubator). First, we install the module with an npm command:

```
> npm install --save bs-webapi
```

Then, we put it in the bs-dependencies section of file bsconfig.json:

```
webpage/shirts/bsconfig.json
// This is the configuration file used by BuckleScript's build system bsb.
// Its documentation lives here:
// http://bucklescript.github.io/bucklescript/docson/#build-schema.json
// BuckleScript comes with its own parser for bsconfig.json, which is normal
// JSON, with the extra support of comments and trailing commas.
{
  "name": "shirts",
  "version": "0.1.0",
  "sources": {
    "dir" : "src",
    "subdirs" : true
  },
  "package-specs": {
    "module": "commonjs",
    "in-source": true
  },
  "suffix": ".bs.js",
  "bs-dependencies": [
      // add your dependencies here. You'd usually install them normally
      // through `npm install my-dependency`. If my-dependency has a
      // bsconfig.json too, then everything will work seamlessly.
      "bs-webapi"
  ],
  "warnings": {
    "error" : "+101"
  },
  "namespace": true,
  "refmt": 3
}
```

Unlike the previous projects where we've used node to run the program from the command line, here we're creating a web page that could live on a server. To tie our code and the HTML file together, we need a *bundler*. A bundler takes the JavaScript code that our ReasonML generated, the code from the ReasonML/BuckleScript libraries that our code uses, and any CSS or image files that might be in our application, making them into a set of files that can be run from a web server or opened in a browser. In this book, I'm using the Parcel bundler, which is very fast and requires a minimum amount of setup (parceljs.org/getting_started.html). Another very popular bundler is webpack (webpack.js.org/). You may, of course, use any other bundler that you are already familiar with.

Accessing the DOM

We're going to be using parts of the Webapi.Dom module a lot, so we'll set up some *module aliases* to avoid repetitive typing:

webpage/shirts/src/WebShirts.re
```
module D = Webapi.Dom;
module Doc = Webapi.Dom.Document;
module Elem = Webapi.Dom.Element;
```

Why use D instead of Dom as the alias for Webapi.Dom? Though it would be more readable, using Dom hides the declaration of the built-in Dom module, which we'll use when we're dealing with events. You'll learn much more about modules in Chapter 7, Structuring Data with Records and Modules, on page 103.

Our first task is to set up a click event handler on the button, which means we have to call getElementById().

```
let calcButton = Doc.getElementById("calculate", D.document);
```

In JavaScript, the DOM version of getElementById() can return null. The bs-webapi function Doc.getElementById() returns an option(Dom.element). Once we call this function, we're in option-land, and we'll stay there as long as possible.

Next, we add a click event listener to the button with addEventListener from the Webapi.Dom.EventTarget module (using the module alias D):

```
switch (calcButton) {
  | Some(element) =>
      D.EventTarget.addEventListener(
        "click", calculate, Elem.asEventTarget(element))
  | None => ()
};
```

Reminder: the vertical bars in the switch introduce the alternatives for the pattern match.

Specific Event Listeners

 We also could have used the addClickEventListener() method from the Dom.EventTarget module and omitted the "click" parameter. The Dom.EventTarget module has a whole host of such pre-declared functions for the most common events. Thus, instead of addEventListener("somename", function, target), you can write addSomeNameEventListener(function, target), where somename is the event you are listening for. There is also a corresponding set of remove...EventListener() functions.

---

addEventListener() returns unit, so the None branch must also return (), which is how we write a value of type unit.

ReasonML requires us to define functions before we use them, so we have to place the calculate() event handler function before the switch expression. For now, this will be a placeholder to let us know that things are working:

```
let calculate = (_: Dom.event) : unit => {
  Js.log("You clicked me!");
};
```

Event handlers have one argument of type Dom.event and return unit. In this program, we don't need any of the information in the event object (the parameter), so we use an underscore to indicate we aren't using it. If we had put in a parameter name, the compiler would complain about an unused variable.

In this code, for the return value, we get lucky—Js.log() returns unit, so we don't need to return () ourselves.

Building the Web Bundle

If we try to use node to run the compiled code, it won't work. Since the program isn't running in a web context, it won't be able to find the Calculate button. We have to use a bundler to make our code and HTML web-ready.

One part of our workflow hasn't changed—we use npm run build to compile the program:

```
> npm run build

 shirts@0.1.0 build /home/you/code/webpage/shirts
 bsb -make-world

[156/156] Building src/canvas/Canvas2dRe.mlast.d
[78/78] Building src/Webapi.cmj
ninja: Entering directory `lib/bs'
[3/3] Building src/WebShirts.mlast.d
[1/1] Building src/WebShirts-Shirts.cmj
```

Here's where we depart from our previous workflow—we use parcel to bundle our files:

```
> parcel build src/index.html --public-url ./ --no-minify
✧  Built in 490ms.

dist/WebShirts.bs.182bc817.js     169.99 KB     195ms
dist/index.html                      734 B        5ms
```

The --public-url sets the public URL from which bundled files will be served. In this case, ./ indicates that the bundled JavaScript will be in the same folder as the HTML. We use --no-minify to see the generated JavaScript in a readable form—the default is to minify the output.

The bundled JavaScript goes into the dist directory. Every time you build, Parcel creates a unique file name (the 182bc817 in the preceding output) for your JavaScript. You may want to periodically clear out the directory or remove it entirely so these files don't accumulate.

Now you can go into the browser, open the web console, and open file dist/index.html. Click the Calculate button, and you should see a message in the console window:

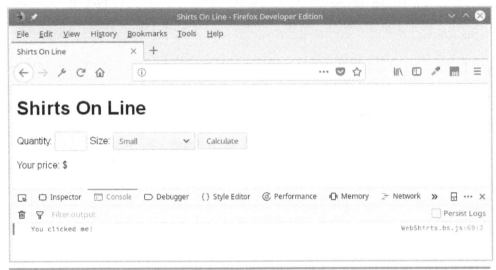

Serving a Bundle

If you use the command parcel src/index.html, Parcel will bundle the JavaScript for you and start Parcel's built-in development server. You can open the browser and go to URL http://localhost:1234 to get the files served up to you.

Completing the Calculation

Now that we know we can get to an element and detect a click, we can expand the calculate() function to:

- Retrieve the values from the quantity and shirt size fields—these will be option(string) values.

- Convert the quantity to option(int).

- Calculate the price, yielding an option(float).

- Convert the result to a string (the empty string if we have a None result).

- Put the string into the <span id="price">.

There are steps where things could go wrong: we might not be able to find the elements for the fields or convert the quantity string to an integer. This means we need option variables throughout, and this is where many JavaScript programmers rebel at the cognitive burden of figuring out which Belt.Option functions to use in order to pass values along properly.

If you're at the point of rebellion (or slight dread) at the thought, please consider this a classic "pay now or pay later" problem. ReasonML asks us to pay now with the use of option, with the possibility of type errors discovered at compile time. JavaScript asks us to pay later by tracking down runtime null and undefined errors. In my experience, "pay later" almost always turns out to be far more expensive, so let's start to "pay now."

Getting a Value

getElementById() gives us a value of type option(Webapi.Dom.Element.t), where the t stands for "type." This is a generic element. It is the "parent" of more specific types of elements such as HTML elements or SVG elements, and its interface doesn't include any functions for obtaining an element's value= attribute. The interface for HTML elements *does* have such a function. Since we are dealing with an HTML element, we'll use unsafeAsHtmlElement() to tell ReasonML to treat this element as an HTML element.

Why is it Called Unsafe?

The function name unsafeAsHtmlElement() contains unsafe because it calls JavaScript directly and will work on any element, even one that is not specifically an HTML element. In terms used by object-oriented programming languages, you could say we are *downcasting* an Element to the HtmlElement subclass.

In this code, we use the module alias Elem for Webapi.Dom.Element (we established this alias at the beginning of the section on accessing the DOM on page 49). The t in Elem.t is a convention used when defining types in ReasonML. You can read it as "element type":

```
let getValue = (element: option(Elem.t)) : option(string) => {
  let htmlElement = Belt.Option.map(element, Elem.unsafeAsHtmlElement);
  Belt.Option.map(htmlElement, D.HtmlElement.value);
};
```

We can use pipe first, as described on page 44 to rewrite getValue() as follows:

```
webpage/shirts/src/WebShirts.re
let getValue = (element: option(Elem.t)) : option(string) => {
  element
    -> Belt.Option.map(_, Elem.unsafeAsHtmlElement)
    -> Belt.Option.map(_, D.HtmlElement.value);
};
```

Converting to Integer

The built-in int_of_string() function throws an exception if we give it bad data. This code: let x = int_of_string("blah"); produces the following in the web console:

```
uncaught exception: Failure,-2,int_of_string
```

If we know the details of an exception, we can process it in a switch expression:

webpage/shirts/src/WebShirts.re
```
let toInt = (s:string): option(int) => {
  switch (int_of_string(s)) {
    | result => Some(result)
    | exception(Failure("int_of_string")) => None
  }
};
```

We now have a function that returns a well-behaved option rather than throwing an exception that sends our program into oblivion.

Getting the Quantity and Unit Price

Using the shirtSizeOfString() function that we developed on page 38, we have all the tools we need to get the information from the quantity and size fields:

webpage/shirts/src/WebShirts.re
```
let quantity = getValue(Doc.getElementById("quantity", D.document))
  -> Belt.Option.flatMap(_, toInt);

let unitPrice = getValue(Doc.getElementById("size", D.document))
  -> Belt.Option.flatMap(_, shirtSizeOfString)
  -> Belt.Option.map(_, price);
```

Writing It Out Completely

If you're still uncomfortable with Belt.Option.map() and Belt.Option.flatMap(), here's the code expanded into switch expressions:

```
let quantity =
  switch (getValue(Doc.getElementById("quantity", D.document))) {
    | Some(vQty) => toInt(vQty)
    | None => None
  };
let unitPrice =
  switch(getValue(Doc.getElementById("size", D.document))) {
    | Some(vSize) =>
        switch (shirtSizeOfString(vSize)) {
          | Some(sSize) => Some(price(sSize))
          | None => None
        }
    | None => None
  };
```

Let's stop, take a deep breath, and figure out where we are right now. quantity is bound to an option(int). If we'd entered 5 into the quantity field in the HTML form, the value would be Some(5). If we'd entered five, the value would be None.

Similarly, unitPrice is bound to an option(float). If we'd selected Medium from the drop-down menu, the value would be Some(12.50). If we'd messed up our <select> menu to include an invalid <option> tag, the value would be None.

Calculating the Total Price

Okay cool. We have an option(int) for quantity and option(float) for unit price. If they're both Some(...) values, we're good to go. In any other case, at least one of them is a None and our result has to be None.

We need a switch expression—but we have two values, and doing a nested switch would make our code clunky and hard to read. ReasonML very conveniently allows us to use destructuring in a switch on multiple variables, which are enclosed in parentheses—the uPrice and qty in the following code:

```
webpage/shirts/src/WebShirts.re
let totalPrice = switch (unitPrice, quantity) {
  | (Some(uPrice), Some(qty)) => Some(uPrice *. float_of_int(qty))
  | (_, _) => None
};
```

In this code, the first switch case tries matching against two Some() variables, and if they match, we return the calculated price wrapped up in Some(). The second switch case matches everything else—the underscores denoting that we don't care what their values are. At least one of them must be a None, and we pass it along.

It's time to convert the totalPrice to a string, which lets us emerge from option-land. If at any point we've generated a None, we'll convert it to the empty string.

```
webpage/shirts/src/WebShirts.re
let priceString = switch (totalPrice) {
  | Some(total) => Js.Float.toFixedWithPrecision(total, ~digits=2)
  | None => ""
};
```

Setting HTML Text

The final step is to take that string and place it into the inner text of the <span id="price"> with setInnerText(). We need to use Belt.Option.map() because Doc.getElementById() returns an option. We bind the result to _ on the left-hand side because we don't need to use the result for any further calculation.

```
webpage/shirts/src/WebShirts.re
let _ = Doc.getElementById("price", D.document)
  -> Belt.Option.map(_, Elem.setInnerText(_, priceString));

(); /* return unit */
```

There are two underscores on the right-hand side, and they serve very different purposes. The first underscore after Belt.Option.Map() tells pipe first where to put the option(Element). The second underscore takes a bit more explanation. The setInnerText() function has two parameters: the element and the desired text, but Belt.Option.Map() wants a function with one parameter. Just as we did in our discussion of Belt.Option on page 43, we use partial application to solve this problem. The underscore in the setInnerText() call skips the first positional parameter and partially applies the priceString.

Let's look at the calculate() function all together so we can see the big picture of the code:

```
webpage/shirts/src/WebShirts.re
let calculate = (_: Dom.event) : unit => {
  let quantity = getValue(Doc.getElementById("quantity", D.document))
    -> Belt.Option.flatMap(_, toInt);

  let unitPrice = getValue(Doc.getElementById("size", D.document))
    -> Belt.Option.flatMap(_, shirtSizeOfString)
    -> Belt.Option.map(_, price);

  let totalPrice = switch (unitPrice, quantity) {
    | (Some(uPrice), Some(qty)) => Some(uPrice *. float_of_int(qty))
    | (_, _) => None
  };

  let priceString = switch (totalPrice) {
    | Some(total) => Js.Float.toFixedWithPrecision(total, ~digits=2)
    | None => ""
  };

  let _ = Doc.getElementById("price", D.document)
    -> Belt.Option.map(_, Elem.setInnerText(_, priceString));

  (); /* return unit */
};
```

It's Your Turn

1. Modify the shirts program to add change event listeners to the input text field and the select menu. (You may want to add an input listener to the text field if you want to update the results with every keypress.) If you wish, you can get rid of the Calculate button, which will no longer be necessary. One solution is in the code/webpage/shirtchange/src directory.

2. Write a program to calculate monthly loan payments. Here's an HTML page you can use as a starting point. There is no Calculate button, so you'll want to have onchange handlers for the input fields, all of which call your calculation function.

```
webpage/loan/src/index.html
<!DOCTYPE html>
<html>
<head>
  <title>Monthly Payment Calculator</title>
  <meta http-equiv="Content-Type" content="text/html; charset=utf-8" />
  <style type="text/css">
    p { margin-top: 0.5em; margin-bottom: 0.5em; }
  </style>
</head>

<body>
  <h1>Monthly Payment Calculator</h1>

  <p>
  Principal: $ <input type="text" size="10" id="principal"/>
  </p>
  <p>
  Annual Percentage Rate: <input type="text" size="7" id="apr"/> %
  </p>
  <p>
  Number of years: <input type="text" size="4" id="years"/>
  </p>

  <p>
  Your monthly payment is $<span id="payment"></span>
  </p>

  <script type="text/javascript" src="LoanPayment.bs.js"></script>
</body>
</html>
```

The principal and annual percentage rate should be float, while the number of years should be int. Here's the code for computing the monthly payments:

```
functions/src/LabeledParams.re
let payment = (~principal, ~apr, ~years) => {
  let r = apr /. 12.0 /. 100.0;
  let n = float_of_int(years * 12);
  let powerTerm = (1.0 +. r) ** n;
  principal *. (r *. powerTerm) /. (powerTerm -. 1.0);
};
```

Remember to include bs-webapi in the bs-dependencies section of the project's bsconfig.json file. You may also want to write utility functions to make your code more readable:

```
let getIntValue = (elementId: string) : option(int) => {...}
let getFloatValue = (elementId: string) : option(float) => {...}
```

Bad data will give a Failure("float_of_string") exception when converting from string to float. Your code should catch this and produce a None, much as we did in the toInt() function. One solution is in the code/webpage/loan/src directory.

Reviewing DOM Functions

Here are the signatures of the DOM access functions we've used in this chapter, plus a couple that you might find useful in working with the DOM:

Webapi.Dom.Document.getElementById: string => option(Dom.Element) Given a string, this function returns a DOM element wrapped in Some(), or None if the ID isn't found.

Webapi.Dom.Element.asEventTarget: Dom.Element.t => Dom.eventTarget This function takes a DOM element and returns it in a form that can have an event attached to it.

Webapi.Dom.EventTarget.addEventListener: (string, Dom.event => unit, Dom.eventTarget) => unit This function takes an event name as a string and a handler function to call when the event occurs. This function returns unit. The event handler (the second argument) is a function that takes a Dom.event as its parameter and returns unit.

Webapi.Dom.Element.unsafeAsHtmlElement: Webapi.Dom.Element.t => Dom.htmlElement This function takes a DOM element and returns it in a form that allows it to be treated as an HTML element.

Webapi.Dom.HtmlElement.value: Webapi.Dom.HtmlElement.t_htmlElement => string This function takes an HTML element as its parameter and returns its value= as a string.

Webapi.Dom.Element.innerText: Webapi.Dom.Element.t => string This function takes an Element and returns the text inside it as a string.

Webapi.Dom.Element.setInnerText: (Webapi.Dom.Element.t, string) => unit This function sets the text inside the given Element to the given string, and returns unit.

Webapi.Dom.Element.getAttribute: (string, Webapi.Dom.Element.t) => option(string) This function retrieves the value of the given attribute (the first parameter) of the given Element, wrapped in Some(), if the attribute exists for the element. If the element doesn't have the required attribute, the function returns None.

Webapi.Dom.Element.setAttribute: (string, string, Webapi.Dom.Element.t) => unit This function takes three parameters: the name of an attribute, the value you want it to have, and the Element that owns the attribute. It sets the attribute to the given value and returns unit.

Summing Up

You now know how to use bs-webapi to interact with a web page by getting an element by its id attribute, attaching an event listener to a button, retrieving a form value, and setting an element's text. You've seen how we can use Belt.Option.map() and Belt.Option.flatMap() to handle invalid data in a type-safe way without null or undefined issues.

bs-webapi is fairly low-level—if you use it a great deal, you'll find yourself writing utility functions to handle common situations. Eventually, you may want to create a full-blown single-page application. ReasonML is very tightly integrated with React (reactjs.org/), as you'll see in Chapter 9, Making Applications with Reason/React, on page 141.

Before we get there, though, we have to finish discussing some aspects of ReasonML that will come up in many programs, not just web apps. We'll examine one of these in the next chapter—the ability to process collections of data such as tuples, lists, and arrays.

CHAPTER 5

Using Collections

In this chapter, we'll investigate three ways to handle multiple, related pieces of data: tuples, lists, and arrays:

- Tuples let you collect items with different data types. They usually hold only a few items.

- Lists have elements that are all of the same data type, and are meant to be traversed from beginning to end.

- Array elements also must be of the same data type, but they allow efficient random access to the elements.

For lists and arrays, we'll learn about the Belt.List and Belt.Array modules, which contain a large number of functions that make it easier to manipulate these collections. We will also start using three very important higher-order functions: map(), reduce(), and keep(). Combining these functions lets you manipulate lists and arrays without using for loops, resulting in shorter code that's easier to read.

Accessing Functions in Other Files

We're going to be using the shirt size data type and its associated functions from Chapter 3, Creating Your Own Data Types, on page 29 for several of the examples—and it would be nice to not have to duplicate that code to each of the files. Before getting into the discussion of collections, we can do some housekeeping and solve that problem. First, create a project:

```
you@computer:~/book_projects> bsb -init collections -theme basic-reason
Making directory collections
Symlink bs-platform in /home/you/book_projects/collections
you@computer:~/book_projects> cd collections
```

and put all the shirt size handling code into one file. Let's rename some of the functions to make typing and readability easier, and remove the option from the price() function, like this:

collections/src/ShirtSize.re

```
type shirtSize =
  | Small
  | Medium
  | Large
  | XLarge(int);

type t = shirtSize;

let price = (size: shirtSize) : float => {
  switch (size) {
    | Small => 11.00
    | Medium => 12.50
    | Large => 14.00
    | XLarge(n) => 16.00 +. (float_of_int(n - 1) *. 0.50)
  }
};
let toString = (size: shirtSize) : string => {
  switch (size) {
    | Small => "S"
    | Medium => "M"
    | Large => "L"
    | XLarge(n) => String.make(n, 'X') ++ "L"
  };
};
let fromString = (str: string) : option(shirtSize) => {
  switch (str) {
    | "S" => Some(Small)
    | "M" => Some(Medium)
    | "L" => Some(Large)
    | "XL" => Some(XLarge(1))
    | "XXL" => Some(XLarge(2))
    | "XXXL" => Some(XLarge(3))
    | "XXXXL" => Some(XLarge(4))
    | _ => None
  }
};
let toFixed = Js.Float.toFixedWithPrecision;
```

This file is now a module, and you can access its data type and functions from the Demo.re file by qualifying the names with the module name ShirtSize:

collections/src/Demo.re

```
let myShirt = ShirtSize.XLarge(1);

let myPrice = ShirtSize.price(myShirt);

Js.log(ShirtSize.toFixed(myPrice, ~digits=2)); /* output: 16.00 */
```

One important addition we've made in the module is this type alias:

```
type t = shirtSize;
```

This is a convention in ReasonML programs. The t stands for *type*, which lets us annotate parameters or variables as ShirtSize.t (read as *ShirtSize type*) instead of the longer and less readable ShirtSize.shirtSize. We'll talk more about modules in Chapter 7, Structuring Data with Records and Modules, on page 103.

Grouping Heterogeneous Data with Tuples

The simplest form of collection is the *tuple*, which consists of a series of values in parentheses. The classic example of a tuple is for use as a pair of (*x*, *y*) coordinates:

collections/src/Coordinates.re
```
type coord = (float, float);

let distance = (p0: coord, p1: coord) : float => {
  let (x0, y0) = p0;
  let (x1, y1) = p1;
  sqrt((x0 -. x1) ** 2.0 +. (y0 -. y1) ** 2.0)
};

let startPoint = (3.5, 4.6);
let endPoint = (0.5, 9.6);
let result = distance(startPoint, endPoint);
Js.log(result);  /* output: 5.830951894845301 */
```

Pay special attention to the let bindings in the distance() function. They use destructuring to extract the elements of the tuple into separate bindings for each element of the tuple. So in the first statement, x0 is bound to the first element of p0 and y0 to the second element.

Another way we *could* have written this code is by using the fst() and snd() functions, which return the first and second element of a tuple that has exactly two elements (a two-tuple):

collections/src/Coordinates.re
```
let distance2 = (p0: coord, p1: coord) : float => {
  let x0 = fst(p0);
  let y0 = snd(p0);
  let x1 = fst(p1);
  let y1 = snd(p1);
  sqrt((x0 -. x1) ** 2.0 +. (y0 -. y1) ** 2.0)
};
```

Using fst() and snd()

 I don't recommend becoming enamored of these two functions. First, they can make your code longer and more difficult to read. Second, fst() and snd() work *only* with two-tuples. They're only here in the book for the sake of completeness, as you may encounter them in your travels through ReasonML-land.

One of the nice things about tuples is they don't have to have the same type of data in each element. In this chapter, we're going to be working with two-tuples that represent an order for shirts. The first element of the tuple tells how many have been ordered and the second element tells which size was ordered:

collections/src/Order.re
```
type order = (int, ShirtSize.t);

let order1 = (3, ShirtSize.Medium);
let order2 = (5, ShirtSize.XLarge(3));
```

We'll need a function that converts an order to a string:

collections/src/Order.re
```
let toString = ((qty, size): order) : string =>
  string_of_int(qty) ++ " " ++ ShirtSize.toString(size);

Js.log(toString(order1)); /* 3 M */
Js.log(toString(order2)); /* 5 XXXL */
```

Hey, I just sneaked in something new. I'm destructuring the order parameter in the function declaration. This is perfectly legal, and it's a nifty trick for making your code shorter.

Using Lists

To create a list, you um... list the elements within square brackets. Unlike tuples, whose elements may be of different types, a list's elements must all have the same type. Lists in ReasonML are *immutable*. Once you create a list, you can't change the contents of an individual element. Instead, all of the list manipulation functions we'll look at return a brand-new list. Let's create and display a short list of integers:

collections/src/IntList.re
```
let example = [10, 11, 12];
Js.log(example);
```

With this rather surprising result:

```
you@computer:~/book_projects/collections> node src/IntList.bs.js
[ 10, [ 11, [ 12, 0 ] ] ]
```

What we're seeing is a reflection of the internal form of a list. If we had more than three elements in the list, we'd see the word Array (or Object, depending on which JavaScript engine is in use) to represent the remaining elements. Luckily, we'll never have to deal directly with this internal representation, but here are two consequences of the internal representation (and the fact that we are dealing with them in a functional setting):

1. Lists are designed to be processed from beginning to end. Accessing a single element in the middle of a list is possible, but it's not an extremely efficient operation.

2. When you add an element to a list, it is added at the *beginning* of the list, not the end.

Manipulating Lists with Belt.List

The Belt.List module defines a large number of functions for processing lists. (Just a note: the Belt.List definitions and examples[1] are written in OCaml format.) We'll use the following list for many of the examples:

collections/src/ListExamples.re
```
let items = [10, 11, 12, 13, 14, 15, 16];
```

For example, the length() function returns the number of elements in the list, so length(items) returns 7. You can use size() as a synonym for length().

This section is going to be somewhat of a laundry list of utility functions because it's difficult to find a specific example that uses all of them. (It's not an exhaustive list. See the documentation for that.) To make it easier to read, I'll avoid prefacing each function name with Belt.List in the explanation.

Creating Lists and Adding Elements to Lists

If you need a list consisting of an element repeated many times, use make(). For example make(5, 7.0) returns the list [7.0, 7.0, 7.0, 7.0, 7.0]

The more versatile makeBy() function takes the number of repetitions as its first argument (call it n) and a function as its second argument. That function will be called with the numbers 0 through n - 1, and the results of that function will populate the list. For example, if we want a list of the square roots of 1 through 5, we would write code like this:

---

1. bucklescript.github.io/bucklescript/api/Belt.List.html

collections/src/ListExamples.re

```
let sqrtPlusOne = (x) => { sqrt(float_of_int(x) +. 1.0) };
let roots = Belt.List.makeBy(5, sqrtPlusOne);
```

This gives the result [1., 1.41421356237, 1.73205080757, 2., 2.2360679775].

As mentioned, adding an element to a list adds it at the start (also called the *head*) of the list. You can add a 9 to the start of the items list either with the add() function or by using notation reminiscent of JavaScript's spread syntax —see the section titled *Spread in array literals* on the MDN Web Docs site:[2]

collections/src/ListExamples.re

```
let added1 = Belt.List.add(items, 9);
let added2 = [9, ...items];
```

If you need to join two lists, use concat(). The following code will result in [10, 11, 12, 13, 14, 15, 16, 17, 18, 19]:

collections/src/ListExamples.re

```
let more = [17, 18, 19];
let joined = Belt.List.concat(items, more);
```

Splitting Lists

The two most-used functions for splitting a list are head() and tail(), which return the first element in a list and the remaining elements in the list, respectively. In this case, head(items) returns 10, and tail(items) returns [11, 12, 13, 14, 15, 16].

If you want the first n elements of a list, use take(). To get everything *except* the first n elements, use drop(). These functions return an option type, and they return None if the number of elements you request is negative or greater than the number of elements in the list:

collections/src/ListExamples.re

```
let taken3 = Belt.List.take(items, 3); /* Some([10, 11, 12]) */
let dropped3 = Belt.List.drop(items, 3); /* Some([13, 14, 15, 16]) */
let badTake = Belt.List.take(items, 10); /* None */
```

The splitAt(items, n) function returns an option two-tuple. If successful, the first element in the tuple is a list of the first n list elements, and the second element in the tuple is a list of the remaining elements. If n is negative or greater than the number of elements in the list, splitAt() returns None:

---

2. developer.mozilla.org/en-US/docs/Web/JavaScript/Reference/Operators/Spread_syntax

```
collections/src/ListExamples.re
let result = Belt.List.splitAt(items, 3);
switch (result) {
  | Some((firstPart, lastPart)) => {
      Js.log(firstPart); /* [10, 11, 12] */
      Js.log(lastPart); /* [13, 14, 15, 16] */
    }
  | None => Js.log("None")
};
```

Accessing Individual List Elements

Belt.List provides two functions for extracting a single element from a list: get() and getExn(). Both of these functions take the index of the element you want as their argument, with zero being the first element in the list. get() returns an option value—Some(value) if the index is within the bounds of the list, None otherwise.

If you don't want to deal with option or you enjoy living dangerously, use getExn(), which will return the element if the index is valid or will throw a getExn error if the index is invalid.

```
collections/src/ListExamples.re
let optElement = Belt.List.get(items, 3); /* Some(13) */
let badOptElement = Belt.List.get(items, 10); /* None */
let element = Belt.List.getExn(items, 3); /* 13 */
let badElement: int =
  try (Belt.List.getExn(items, 10)) {
  | Js.Exn.Error(e) =>
    switch (Js.Exn.message(e)) {
    | Some(message) => Js.log({j|Error: $message|j}) /* "Error: getExn"*/
    | None => Js.log("An unknown error occurred")
    };
    (-1);
  };
Js.log(badElement);
```

The preceding code uses try—another way of handling exceptions in addition to what we have seen on page 54. If the expression in try succeeds, its value is returned. Otherwise, the Js.Exn.Error() pattern match puts the exception into variable e, allowing us to display the error message (if any). The (-1) at the end of the try structure is there to return an integer (which is what a successful getExn() would return.

Again, these aren't tremendously efficient operations—lists are designed for sequential rather than random access—but if you need them, you have them available.

Using map(), keep(), and reduce() with Lists

Before we get started on this section, you might be having a slight case of *déjà vu*—haven't we already covered map() in the discussion of option on page 42? Yes and no. The plain truth is that the word *map* occurs in a large number of contexts in functional programming. Almost any time you find a construct that's even remotely like the mathematical idea of a function *mapping* a domain onto a range, sure enough, someone has slapped the term *map* onto it. The map() in this section isn't the same as the one you saw before, and—fair warning—it's not the last time you'll see that term pop up in this book.

Now that we've done the housekeeping and laundry, it's time to use list functions to process the data in a list. Consider this list of order tuples:

collections/src/MapKeepReduce.re
```
let orderList = [(7, ShirtSize.Medium), (5, ShirtSize.XLarge(3)),
  (4, ShirtSize.Small), (6, ShirtSize.Large), (8, ShirtSize.Small),
  (2, ShirtSize.Large), (9, ShirtSize.Medium), (3, ShirtSize.XLarge(2))];
```

We'll use the map(), keep(), and reduce() functions to do things like this:

- Determine the price of each order
- Create a new list with only the orders for size Medium
- Figure out the total price for all the orders
- Figure out the total price for the Medium shirts only

There's an important point to be noted here: All of these operations are *transforming* the original list of orders into some new form. In other languages, for the first task, you might use a for loop of the form:

```
priceList = []
for (i = 0; i < orderList.length(); i++) {
  /* calculate price of order and append to priceList */
}
```

for loops won't fly in ReasonML because mutating variables (like i and the price list) is frowned upon. When working in a functional programming language like ReasonML, we take a different approach. We pass the original list to a function like map() and receive a transformed list. This, in turn, can be passed on to other transformations.

Using map()

Let's tackle the first task of creating a list of prices for each order. The map() function takes two parameters: the list to be processed and a function that does the appropriate calculation on a single element. map() will then apply the function to each element in the list, add the result to a new list, and return the new list after all elements are processed. It's probably easier to show you some code:

collections/src/MapKeepReduce.re
```
let onePrice = ((qty: int, size: ShirtSize.t)) : float => {
  float_of_int(qty) *. ShirtSize.price(size);
};

let priceList = Belt.List.map(orderList, onePrice);
```

The onePrice() function takes a single order and returns the total price by multiplying the quantity of shirts by the price per shirt. The call to map() accepts the list of orders and applies onePrice() to each element of orderList. The resulting list, which is bound to priceList, is [87.5, 85., 44., 84., 88., 28., 112.5, 49.5].

Using keep()

The second task, creating a new list consisting of only the Medium shirt orders, is a job for keep(). Like map(), it's a higher-order function. Its first parameter is also the list of elements to be processed. The second parameter is a function, but this function takes an element and returns true if the element is to be added to the result list or false if it won't be kept. This code:

collections/src/MapKeepReduce.re
```
let isMedium = ((_, size)): bool => {
  size === ShirtSize.Medium;
};

let mediums = Belt.List.keep(orderList, isMedium);
```

Produces the list [(7, Medium), (9, Medium)]. In the isMedium() function, the outer parentheses in ((_, size)) delimit the argument list. The inner parentheses denote a two-tuple. The underscore is used to ignore the quantity part of the tuple, as it isn't used in the function body. The body of isMedium() is only one line, so this is a case where it might be better to express it as an anonymous function. We make the anonymous function by using the body of isMedium() (everything to the right of the =). We've also dropped the annotation and braces to save space.

collections/src/MapKeepReduce.re
```
let mediums2 = Belt.List.keep(orderList,
  ((_, size)) => size === ShirtSize.Medium);
```

An anonymous function is a function body that hasn't been bound to a name. In general, anonymous functions tend to be short—most often one or two lines. If the function you're passing to another function is fairly lengthy, it's best to define it as a separate, named function and then pass on the name.

This makes your code more readable. There is a school of thought that says readability should be your primary concern—you and other people will be reading the code more often than the computer will—so you should use named functions instead of anonymous functions, no matter how short they are. In this book I have not subscribed entirely to this philosophy, so you will see quite a few short anonymous functions. Your mileage may vary.

---

keep() in Other Programming Languages

 Many other functional languages use the name filter instead of keep. In English, people think of things being filtered *out*, but the function argument returns true for elements that should be kept *in*. If you ask me, keep is a much more descriptive name for the function.

Using reduce()

The map() function returns a list with the same number of elements as the input list, though the result may be list of a different type than the input. keep() returns a list with (potentially) a different number of elements, but of the same type as the input list. Sometimes you might like to process the list and return a result with a different number of elements and/or a different type. This is the case with our third task: figuring out the total price for all the orders. We want to return a single float from a list of order. The reduce() function lets us do exactly that.

reduce() has three parameters:

- The list to be processed, of type 'a (see What's a Parametric Data Type?, on page 38).

- The starting value of an *accumulator* that will accumulate the function result as elements are processed. It's of type 'b. (It's not of type 'a because reduce() can return a different type than the list type. 'a and 'b might turn out to be the same type, but they don't have to be.)

- The reducer function.

reduce() goes through the input list, one element at a time. For each element, it passes the current value of the accumulator and the element to the reducer function. The reducer function takes those two values and returns the new value for the accumulator. When reduce() has processed all the elements, it returns the current value of the accumulator as its result. Let's look at some code and its output. We've added a call to Js.log() so you can see what is happening, step by step:

```
collections/src/MapKeepReduce.re
let addPriceLogged = (runningTotal, orderItem) => {
  let price = onePrice(orderItem);
  Js.log({j|$runningTotal, $price|j});
  runningTotal +. price;
};

Js.log("Running total / Price")
let totalPrice = Belt.List.reduce(orderList, 0.0, addPriceLogged);
Js.log2("Total price:", totalPrice); /* Total price: 578.5 */

Running total / Price
0, 87.5
87.5, 85
172.5, 44
216.5, 84
300.5, 88
388.5, 28
416.5, 112.5
529, 49.5
Total price: 578.5
```

It's worthwhile to analyze what's happening in this code. This description is for someone who's never used the reduce() function before:

1. The accumulator is set to 0.0.

2. The accumulator and the first element in the list (7, ShirtSize.Medium) are sent to addPrice().

3. addPrice() returns 0.0 (the accumulator) plus 87.50 (the price of seven Medium shirts). This is the new value of the accumulator.

4. reduce() now passes this new value 87.50 and the next element in the list (5, ShirtSize.XLarge(3)) to addPrice().

5. addPrice() returns 87.50 plus 85.00 (the price of five XLarge(3) shirts). The result, 172.50, becomes the new value of the running total (accumulator).

6. reduce() now calls addPrice(172.50, (4, ShirtSize.small)) to process the next elements.

7. addPrice() returns 172.50 plus 44.00 (the price of four Small shirts), which is 216.50.

This continues until the list is totally processed and we get 587.5 as the total price for all our shirt orders.

Without the logging, the code would be written like this:

collections/src/MapKeepReduce.re
```
let addPrice = (runningTotal, orderItem) => {
  runningTotal +. onePrice(orderItem);
};

let totalPrice = Belt.List.reduce(orderList, 0.0, addPrice);
```

Other programming languages use different names like fold() or fold_left() to do what ReasonML calls reduce().

Combining map(), keep(), and reduce()

Each of these functions is quite useful. When combined, they can do wonderful things. For example, you, as a sharp-eyed reader, might have noticed that we already calculated the list of prices for each order on page 69. We could have calculated the grand total price this way:

collections/src/MapKeepReduce.re
```
let addPriceToTotal = (runningTotal, price) => runningTotal +. price;

let totalPrice2 =
  Belt.List.map(orderList, onePrice) ->
  Belt.List.reduce(_, 0.0, addPriceToTotal);
Js.log2("Total price:", totalPrice2); /* Total price: 578.5 */
```

In the preceding code, we used the pipe first operator -> to send the result of calculating the price list (via Belt.List.map()) to Belt.List.reduce(). Though the reducer function is short enough to be expressed as an anonymous function, we have defined addPriceToTotal() to add the price from the calculated list to the accumulator.

Using Operators as Functions

For the true minimalists among you, we could make our reducer function even shorter. In the following code, we put the floating point addition operator +. in parentheses. This tells ReasonML to use it as a function rather than an operator, and it's the function we want: it takes two arguments and returns the result of adding them:

collections/src/MapKeepReduce.re
```
let totalPrice3 =
  Belt.List.map(orderList, onePrice) ->
  Belt.List.reduce(_, 0.0, (+.));
Js.log2("Total price:", totalPrice3); /* Total price: 578.5 */
```

When you're using an operator, the accumulator is the first operand and the list element is the second operand. Thus, this code:

```
let data = [2.0, 4.0, 5.0];
let n = Belt.List.reduce(data, 1.0, (/.))
```

Works out to (((1.0 / 2.0) / 4.0) / 5.0), or 0.025. You may see this sort of notation in other people's code, and you should be able to recognize what it does. However, you don't have to write your code this way. If you're more comfortable with an anonymous function or a named reducer function, then use that instead.

Another example of combining these functions is our final task: figuring out the total price for the Medium shirts only. The logic is: keep() only the Medium shirts (using the previously defined isMedium() predicate function), use map() to calculate the individual prices, and send those to reduce() to add them:

collections/src/MapKeepReduce.re
```
let mediumTotal =
  Belt.List.keep(orderList, isMedium) ->
  Belt.List.map(_, onePrice) ->
  Belt.List.reduce(_, 0.0, addPriceToTotal);
Js.log2("Medium total:", mediumTotal); /* Medium total: 200*/
```

Interlude: Displaying Lists

As we saw at the beginning of this chapter on page 64, the default display of a list leaves much to be desired. If we have a list with more than three elements, we see only the first three and then the word Array (which is odd, given that we have a list rather than array) or Object to indicate that there are more elements. While writing this chapter, though, I needed to see *all* the elements, so I wrote a function named stringOfList to get things done.

The general plan was to use reduce(): the accumulator starts off as the empty string. The reducer function converts a list element to a string and appends it, along with a comma and space, to the accumulator. Here's the code for a list of integers:

collections/src/DisplayList.re
```
let intReducer = (accumulator: string, item: int) => {
  accumulator ++ string_of_int(item) ++ ", ";
};

let stringOfIntList = (items: list(int)): string => {
  "[" ++ Belt.List.reduce(items, "", intReducer)
    ++ "]";
}

let items = [10, 11, 12, 13, 14, 15];
Js.log(stringOfIntList(items));
```

Here's the result of running the program:

```
you@computer:~/book_projects/collections> node src/DisplayList.bs.js
[10, 11, 12, 13, 14, 15, ]
```

That output is definitely more useful. Now, what about a list of floats?

collections/src/DisplayList.re
```
let floatReducer = (accumulator: string, item: float) => {
  accumulator ++ string_of_float(item) ++ ", ";
};

let stringOfFloatList = (items: list(float)): string => {
  "[" ++ Belt.List.reduce(items, "", floatReducer)
    ++ "]";
}

let floatItems = [3.6, 7.9, 8.25, 41.0];
Js.log(stringOfFloatList(floatItems));
```

And its output...

```
you@computer:~/book_projects/collections> node src/DisplayList.bs.js
[3.6, 7.9, 8.25, 41., ]
```

There's a problem brewing here: we're going to need a different display and reducer function (or at least a display function if we decide to go with an anonymous reducer function) for every different data type. This, again, is far from ideal. Instead, we'd like to use a parametric data type as described on page 38. In addition to passing the list, we'll also need to pass in a function that tells us how to convert the elements in that list to a string. The partial code will look like this:

```
let displayList = (items: list('a), stringify: ('a) => string) : string => {
  "[" ++ Belt.List.reduce(items, "", elementReducer) ++ "]";
};

Js.log(displayList(items, string_of_int));
Js.log(displayList(floatItems, string_of_float))
```

This creates another problem. The as-yet-unwritten elementReducer() function will take the accumulator and current element as parameters—but it will also need access to the stringify() function. There are two ways to handle this problem. The first and easier solution is to define elementReducer() inside of displayList(). This will work because ReasonML allows us to define functions within functions, and the inner functions have access to all parameters and variables in the outer function:

```
collections/src/DisplayList.re
let stringOfList = (items: list('a), stringify: ('a) => string) : string => {
  let elementReducer = (accumulator: string, item: 'a) => {
    accumulator ++ stringify(item) ++ ", ";
  };
  "[" ++ Belt.List.reduce(items, "", elementReducer) ++ "]";
};

Js.log(stringOfList(items, string_of_int));
Js.log(stringOfList(floatItems, string_of_float));
```

I'll confess that I didn't think of this easier solution first. Instead, I did it in a slightly more difficult way. I created a function with three parameters: the convert-to-string function, the accumulator, and the item:

```
let conversion = (converter: ('a => string), acc: string, item: 'a) => {
  acc ++ converter(item) ++ ", "
};
```

This function isn't suitable for using with reduce() because it has three parameters. But I can use currying as described on page 24 to partially call conversion() by providing that first argument:

```
let stringOfList = (items: list('a), stringify: (('a) => string)): string => {
  let reducerFcn = conversion(stringify);
  "[" ++ Belt.List.reduce(items, "", reducerFcn) ++ "]";
};
```

Since I've provided one argument to conversion() in the definition of reducerFcn(), that new function now needs two arguments to fulfill its duty: the accumulator and the item. This makes it a perfect fit for Belt.List.reduce().

In either case, I end up with a function that displays all the items in a list, even though the extra comma and space at the end are ugly. (It turns out that the String.concat() function will solve this problem, though it would not have afforded me the opportunity to give another example of reduce() and currying.)

Using Arrays

Arrays are a lot like lists, but there are significant differences. While lists are immutable, arrays can be changed in place. (Whether this is a good idea or not is another question entirely. One school of thought says mutating arrays is a source of errors.) Unlike lists, arrays don't have a performance penalty for random access.

You define an array by placing the elements, separated by commas, between the delimiters [| and |].

```
collections/src/IntArray.re
let items = [|10, 11, 12, 13, 14, 15, 16|];
Js.log(items);
```

Unlike lists, arrays display quite nicely, but they display square brackets [and] rather than the delimiters [| and |] you used when you created the array:

```
you@computer:~/book_projects/collections> node src/IntArray.bs.js
[ 10, 11, 12, 13, 14, 15, 16 ]
```

In this section, we'll look at Belt.Array, which has many of the same functions as Belt.List, except it takes arrays as parameters instead of lists. You can also take advantage of the Js.Array library,[3] which provides many of the capabilities of the JavaScript Array object.[4]

Creating Arrays and Adding Elements to Arrays

The Belt.Array.make() and Belt.Array.makeBy() functions work like their counterparts in Belt.List.

If you need to join two arrays, use concat(). The following code will result in [|10, 11, 12, 13, 14, 15, 16, 17, 18, 19|]:

```
collections/src/ArrayExamples.re
let more = [|17, 18, 19|];
let joined = Belt.Array.concat(items, more);
```

There's no function corresponding to Belt.List.add(), nor can you use the ... notation with arrays. These would be slow operations for arrays, involving reallocation of the entire array. If you want to append a single value to an array (yielding a new array), make an array that contains that single value and use Belt.Array.concat():

```
collections/src/ArrayExamples.re
let part1 = [|"the", "array", "has"|];
let part2 = Belt.Array.concat(part1, [|"more"|]);
Js.log(part2); /* [|"the", "array", "has", "more"|] */
```

Splitting Arrays

Belt.Array has no functions analogous to head(), tail(), take(), drop(), and splitAt() from Belt.List. Instead, Belt.Array has a slice() function which takes two parameters: a starting offset and a length. The function returns a new array with the specified elements.

---

3. bucklescript.github.io/bucklescript/api/Js.Array.html
4. developer.mozilla.org/en-US/docs/Web/JavaScript/Reference/Global_Objects/Array

```
collections/src/ArrayExamples.re
/* items contains [|10, 11, 12, 13, 14, 15, 16|]; */
Js.log(Belt.Array.slice(items, ~offset=1, ~len=3)); /* [|11, 12, 13|] */
Js.log(Belt.Array.slice(items, ~offset=5, ~len=9)); /* [|15, 16|] */
Js.log(Belt.Array.slice(items, ~offset=-3, ~len=2)); /* [|14, 15|] */
Js.log(Belt.Array.slice(items, ~offset=3, ~len=-2)); /* [| |] */
```

If you try to go beyond the end of the array, as in the second line, you get everything up to and including the end of the array. If you specify a negative offset, it counts from the end of the array (thus, -1 is the last element, -2 is the next to last element, etc.). If you specify a negative length, slice() returns an empty array. As this function always returns a valid array, it doesn't need to return an option value.

Here's a quick exercise for you: write functions arrayTake(), arrayDrop() and arraySplitAt() that work by calling Belt.Array.slice(). You can see my solution at code/collections/src/ArrayAnalogs.re.

Accessing Individual Array Elements

Belt.Array provides three functions for extracting a single element from a array: get(), getExn(), and getUnsafe(). All of these functions take the index of the element you want as their argument, with zero being the first element in the array. get() returns an option value—Some(value) if the index is within the bounds of the array, None otherwise.

If you don't want to deal with option, or you simply enjoy living dangerously, use getExn(), which will return the element if the index is valid or will throw a getExn error if the index is invalid. If you *really* want to live dangerously, use the appropriately labeled getUnsafe(), which returns the JavaScript undefined value if the index is out of bounds—with all the lovely runtime errors that go along with that!

You may also use square brackets to access array elements, as in JavaScript. You'll get an out-of-bounds exception if you attempt to go outside the array bounds.

```
collections/src/ArrayExamples.re
let optElement = Belt.Array.get(items, 3); /* Some(13) */
let badOptElement = Belt.Array.get(items, 10); /* None */
let badOptElement2 = Belt.Array.getUnsafe(items, 10); /* undefined */
let element = Belt.Array.getExn(items, 3); /* 13 */
let bracketElement = items[3]; /* 13 */
let badElement = Belt.Array.getExn(items, 10); /* throws error */
```

Using map(), keep(), and reduce() with Arrays

All these functions work precisely as their counterparts in Belt.List do. You can see the examples, adapted to arrays, in file code/collections/src/ArrayMapKeepReduce.re. Rewriting took very little effort beyond a search-and-replace.

Putting Arrays to Work

Time to build another mini web app. We'll let the user enter a comma-separated list of orders in an input field, then we'll calculate and display the price for each order, the total number of shirts, and the total price.

Here's the HTML:

```
collections-app/src/index.html
<!DOCTYPE html>
<html>
<head>
  <title>Shirt Price Calculator</title>
  <meta http-equiv="Content-Type" content="text/html; charset=utf-8" />
  <style type="text/css">
    .right {text-align: right;}
    .center {text-align: center;}
    th, td {border: 1px solid gray; padding: 3px}
  </style>
</head>

<body>
  <h1>Shirt Price Calculator</h1>

  <p>
  Enter list of orders separated by commas:
  </p>

  <p>
  <input type="text" size="40" id="orders"
    placeholder="Example: 3M, 4@XL, 5 S"/>
  <button id="calculate">Calculate</button>
  </p>

  <h2>Results</h2>
  <div id="table"></div>

  <p>Total shirts: <span id="totalShirts"></span></p>
  <p>Total price: $<span id="totalPrice"></span></p>

  <script type="text/javascript" src="OrderPage.bs.js"></script>
</body>
</html>
```

For example, if someone entered 2@M, 7Q, 6XXL in the text field, the output would read something like the table on page 79.

Quantity	Size	Price
2	M	$25.00
Bad input 7Q		
6	XXL	$96.00

Total number of shirts: 8
Total price: $121.00

Parsing the Input

Let's hold off on the web interaction for now and instead concentrate on the processing we need to do. We'll use *regular expressions*[5] to analyze the input string and split it into individual orders. Here's the plan, presuming an input string of "2@M, 7Q, 6 XXL":

First, split the string using commas as delimiters. This produces an array: [|"2@M", "7Q", "6 XXL"|]. Then use a regular expression to split each item into digits and a size string such a "2" and "M". These strings can be converted to an integer and shirtSize, then combined into an order tuple.

What happens when we get to the bad order 7Q? Your first thought might be to create an option(order) to handle errors. But when we output the table, we would like to show the original data in an error message so users can see their input was invalid, and None (our "error" condition) doesn't store any information. The Belt library anticipates this sort of situation with the Belt.Result library. It's designed for representing the result of an operation that can either succeed or fail, when you need to have data for each case. Its definition looks like this:

```
type t('a, 'b) =
  | Ok(a)
  | Error(b)
```

The definition uses two different algebraic data types, so the Ok variant can hold a different data type than the Error variant. When we get a good string like 6 XXL, the Ok variant will hold an order—Ok((6, XLarge(2)). When we get a bad string like 7Q, we'll create an Error("7Q"). That way, our code for handling errors has access to the original string that caused the error.

The plan, then, is for our program to take the input string and give us an array of Belt.Result orders, which we may process with map(), keep(), and reduce() to produce the data for the web page.

---

5. developer.mozilla.org/en-US/docs/Web/JavaScript/Guide/Regular_Expressions

---

Confession Time

The first time I wrote this code, I *did* use an option type and wrote that it "just felt right" to use it. Only when I started creating the HTML table did I realize I didn't have the original string information. That meant I would have to re-parse the input string in order to display it in the table. I had to solve the problem in a more efficient way. Belt.Result is that other way.

I then rewrote the code and rewrote the explanation to make it appear as if I had anticipated the problem from the very start (and make you think I'm a very clever person indeed).

The moral of the story really is, as Fred Brooks wrote in *The Mythical Man Month*, "plan to throw one away." If you have painted yourself into a corner, feel free to tear the code apart and rewrite. Like confession, it's good for the soul.

Here's the code for splitting on commas:

collections-app/src/OrderPage.re
```
let commaSplit = (s: string) : array(string) => {
  let pattern = [%re "/\\s*,\\s*/"];
  Js.String.splitByRe(pattern, s) ->
    Belt.Array.map(_, (item) => {
      Belt.Option.getWithDefault(item, "")
    })
};
```

You create a regular expression with the form [%re "patternString"]. If your pattern contains backslashes, you must put two of them in a row so that ReasonML will treat them as a true backslash rather than an escape character. Alternatively, you may use this quoting format: {|/\s*,\s*/|} to avoid double backslashes. The pattern: \s*,\s* means "zero or more spaces, followed by a comma, followed by zero or more spaces." Using \s* makes the pattern match more flexible by allowing users to input any number of spaces before or after the commas. Js.String.splitByRe()—the Split By Regular Expression function—returns an array of option delimited strings. If the delimiter pattern isn't in the input string, it returns an array with a single option entry (the entire string). Here's an example:

```
let pattern = [%re "/\\s*,\\s*/"];

Js.String.splitByRe(pattern, "ab, cd , ef, gh"));
/* result: [|Some("ab"), Some("cd"), Some("ef"), Some("gh")|] */

Js.String.splitByRe(pattern, "no commas"));
/* result: [|Some("no commas")|] */
```

We have to change this array of option values to normal values. To do this, we pipe the results of splitByRe() to Belt.Array.map() and use Belt.Option.getWithDefault() in our mapping function. If given Some(value), getwithDefault() returns the value inside the Some. If given None, it returns a default value (in our case, the empty string).

Here's the code for parsing one of the items as an order:

collections-app/src/OrderPage.re

```
Line 1  type order = (int, ShirtSize.t);
        type resultOrder = Belt.Result.t(order, string)

        let orderFromCaptures = (optCaptures: option(array(string)),
     5                            input: string): resultOrder => {
          switch (optCaptures) {
            | Some(captures) => {
                switch (ShirtSize.fromString(captures[2])) {
                  | Some(size) => Belt.Result.Ok((int_of_string(captures[1]), size))
    10            | None => Belt.Result.Error(input)
                }
              }
            | None => Belt.Result.Error(input)
          }
    15  };

        let toOrder = (input: string) : resultOrder => {
          let pattern = [%re "/(\\d{1,4})\\s*@?\\s*(S|M|X{0,4}L)/"];
          Js.String.toUpperCase(input)
    20    -> Js.String.match(pattern, _)
          -> orderFromCaptures(input)
        };
```

Wow. There's a lot to unpack here. The first type definition says an order is a tuple of an integer and a ShirtSize.t. The type definition resultOrder is a type alias for a Belt.Result.t (the t, again, is the ReasonML convention for "type") that will have an order as its Ok variant and a string as its Error variant. It's here mostly to make the annotations, such as the one in the first line of toOrder(), (line 17) easier to read.

Next, the regular expression bound to pattern (line 18):

- (\d{1,4}): one to four digits. If you need more than 9,999 shirts in a single order, you're out of luck. The parentheses tell the regular expression engine to store the matched substring. This is also called a *capture*.

- \s*: zero or more spaces.

- @?: an optional at sign.

- \s*: zero or more spaces.

- (S|M|X{0,4}L): The vertical bars separate alternatives. Match S, M, or zero to four occurrences of the letter X followed by L. This last will match L, XL, XXL, etc. Again, parentheses mean that we want the matching substring stored.

The result of Js.String.match() is Some(array(string)) if the pattern matches, None otherwise. In the case of a match, the first element of the array is the entire matched substring, and the subsequent elements are the matches from the parenthesized portions of the pattern. Matching the pattern against "5 XL" will result in Some([|"5 XL", "5", "XL"|]). The match result is sent to orderFromCaptures() (line 21)

Let's look at the Some(captures) case in line 7 when the pattern matches. The third element in the array, arr[2], is the shirt size as a string, which we must convert to our ShirtSize.t type. Even though the regular expression has guaranteed that the size will be a valid string, the function that does this conversion returns option(ShirtSize.t), so we need an inner switch in line 8 to handle that. The success result is the expression Belt.Result.Ok((int_of_string(captures[1]), size)).

Calculating the Totals

Okay. We now have an array of Belt.Result.t(order, string). We use reduce() to get the total number of shirts. The reducer function adder() adds the number of shirts to the accumulator if the item is Belt.Result.Ok and does no processing of anything else (which would be Belt.Result.Error entries) by passing on the accumulator unchanged:

collections-app/src/OrderPage.re
```
let calculateTotalShirts = (orders: array(resultOrder)): int => {
  let adder = (accumulator: int, resOrder: resultOrder) => {
    switch (resOrder) {
      | Belt.Result.Ok((n, _)) => accumulator + n
      | _ => accumulator
    }
  };
  Belt.Array.reduce(orders, 0, adder);
};
```

We can then use pipe first to calculate the total number of shirts sold—this is the code I wrote to test the parts:

```
let str = "3M, 5 @ S, 7 BAD, 9 XXL";
let nShirts = commaSplit(str) ->
  Belt.Array.map(_, toOrder) ->
  calculateTotalShirts(_);
Js.log(nShirts); /* 17 */
```

We could write a similar function to calculate the total price, but there would be a fair amount of duplicated code. Let's do something clever—process both the total number of shirts and total price, and return them as a tuple. That means the accumulator must be a tuple as well. In order to keep the code from getting too messy, let's also write a convenience function to calculate the total price for a single order and make the reducer function separate for readability:

```
collections-app/src/OrderPage.re
let orderPrice = ((n, size): order): float => {
  float_of_int(n) *. ShirtSize.price(size);
};

let addOrderTotal = (((totalShirts, totalPrice) as current, orderResult) => {
  switch (orderResult) {
    | Belt.Result.Ok((n, _) as order) => (
        totalShirts + n,
        totalPrice +. orderPrice(order)
      )
    | _ => current
  }
};

let calculateTotals = (orders: array(resultOrder)): (int, float) => {
  Belt.Array.reduce(orders, (0, 0.0), addOrderTotal);
};
```

There's something new here on line 5. We are destructuring the tuple into variables totalShirts and totalPrice (we've done that before), but this time we are adding as current. This binds the variable current to the entire non-destructured tuple, so we can refer to it in line 11 without having to say (totalShirts, totalPrice). We use this same trick in lines 7 and 9 to refer to the entire order.

Creating the Output

We'd like to display the individual orders in table form, with each row giving a quantity, size, and total price. If an order is invalid, that row in the table will give the original data with an error message.

The easiest way to create the table is to set the innerHTML of the <div id="table">, so we'll need a function that changes an OK(order) into the HTML for a table row with the quantity, size, and total price. The function changes an Error(string) into the HTML for a table row containing the string and an error message. It uses the {j|...|j} notation to interpolate variables:

collections-app/src/OrderPage.re

```
/* Create a row from an order */
let createRow = (anOrder: resultOrder): string => {
  switch (anOrder) {
     | Belt.Result.Ok((n, size)) => {
          let totalPrice =
            Js.Float.toFixedWithPrecision(orderPrice((n, size)), ~digits=2);
          let sizeStr = ShirtSize.toString(size);
          {j|<tr><td class="right">$n</td>
             <td class="center">$sizeStr</td>
             <td class="right">\$$totalPrice</td></tr>\n|j}
       }
     | Belt.Result.Error(s) =>
          {j|<tr><td colspan="3">Bad input $s</td></tr>\n|j}
  }
};
```

Now that we can create a single row, we use reduce() to accumulate the strings corresponding to each row, and we put them between the start and end of an HTML <table>:

collections-app/src/OrderPage.re

```
let createTable = (orderArray: array(resultOrder)) : string => {
  let tableBody = Belt.Array.reduce(orderArray, "",
    (accumulator, item) => accumulator ++ createRow(item));

  {j|
<table>
  <thead>
    <tr><th>Quantity</th><th>Size</th><th>Price</th>
  </thead>
  <tbody>
|j} ++ tableBody ++  {j|
  </tbody>
</table>
|j};
};
```

Here's the HTML generated from the string 2@M, 7Q, 6 XXL:

```
<table>
  <thead>
    <tr><td>Quantity</td><td>Size</td><td>Price</td>
  </thead>
  <tbody>
<tr><td class="right">2</td>
           <td class="center">M</td>
           <td class="right">$25.00</td></tr>
<tr><td colspan="3">7Q is not valid</td></tr>
```

```
<tr><td class="right">6</td>
          <td class="center">XXL</td>
          <td class="right">$99.00</td></tr>

  </tbody>
</table>
```

Something you might have noticed: the vast majority of the code is setup, short functions for processing individual elements, and literal strings. The actual processing consists of a few calls to map() or reduce(). This indicates the kind of power they have in making your code clear and compact.

Creating the User Interface

Just as we did in Chapter 4, Interacting with Web Pages, on page 47, we set up module aliases, write a function to get a field's value, and connect the Calculate button to an event handler:

collections-app/src/OrderPage.re
```
module D = Webapi.Dom;
module Doc = Webapi.Dom.Document;
module Elem = Webapi.Dom.Element;

let getValue = (element: option(Elem.t)) : option(string) => {
  element
    -> Belt.Option.map(_, Elem.unsafeAsHtmlElement)
    -> Belt.Option.map(_, D.HtmlElement.value);
};
let calcButton = Doc.getElementById("calculate", D.document);
switch (calcButton) {
  | Some(element) =>
      D.EventTarget.addEventListener(
        "click", calculate, D.Element.asEventTarget(element))
  | None => ()
};
```

And here is the event handler itself:

collections-app/src/OrderPage.re
```
let setInnerHTML = (id: string, htmlString: string) => {
  Doc.getElementById(id, D.document)
  -> Belt.Option.map(Elem.setInnerHTML(_, htmlString))
};

let setInnerText = (id: string, textString: string) => {
  Doc.getElementById(id, D.document)
  -> Belt.Option.map(Elem.setInnerText(_, textString))
};
```

```
let calculate = (_: Dom.event) : unit => {
  switch (getValue(Doc.getElementById("orders", D.document))) {
    | Some(str) => {
        let orderArray = commaSplit(str) ->
          Belt.Array.keep(_, (item) => {item !== ""}) ->
          Belt.Array.map(_, toOrder);

        let (nShirts, grandTotal) = calculateTotals(orderArray);
        let priceString = Js.Float.toFixedWithPrecision(grandTotal, ~digits=2);

        let _ = setInnerHTML("table",createTable(orderArray));
        let _ = setInnerText("totalShirts", string_of_int(nShirts));
        let _ = setInnerText("totalPrice", priceString);
        ()
      }
    | None => ()
  }
};
```

There are a couple of things to note about this code. Rather than passing an option value all the way through the code (because the orders field might not exist), we immediately do a switch at the start of the code. When creating the orderArray, we've added an extra step that uses keep() with an anonymous function to make sure we process only non-empty strings. This lets the code work properly when the user doesn't enter anything in the input field. We have also added utility functions setInnerHTML() and setInnerText() to make the code a bit more readable.

It's Your Turn

Consider a two-tuple of data that gives temperature in degrees Celsius and relative humidity as a percent. Write a program that takes a list (or array—whichever you prefer) of these tuples and calculates:

- The dew point for each tuple, using the formula

$$T_d = T - ((100 - RH)/5)$$

  This formula is the simplest one available; it is fairly accurate for relative humidity over 50%. There are more accurate formulas—if you want to research them and implement one of those instead, be my guest.

- The maximum, minimum, and average dew points

Hint: You can use the built-in min() and max() functions, which return the lesser and greater of their two arguments, or you can use reduce() and keep() with your own predicate functions.

Bonus challenge: for the maximums and minimums, give the element indices where they occur. Display the indices starting with one for the benefit of humans, as opposed to zero, which is for the benefit of programmers. For example, in this data: [(27, 55), (15, 70), (18.3, 58.1))], you might display:

```
Minimum value: 9. (at position 2)
Maximum value: 18. (at position 1)
Average value: 12.3066666667
```

If you wish, create a web page interface for doing these calculations and figure out any representation for input of those tuples that makes sense to you. You can see my solution in the code/collections-dewpoint/src directory.

Summing Up

ReasonML gives you the ability to deal with data *en masse* with tuples, lists, and arrays. You've seen how map(), keep(), and reduce(), either alone or in combination, make it easy for you to transform collections.

In the next chapter, we'll investigate recursion, a technique that lets you fine-tune the processing of collections and simplify the way you express algorithms. You'll also see how recursion solves the problem of the extra comma and space that we saw on on page 75.

CHAPTER 6

Repeating with Recursion

Using map(), reduce(), and keep() takes care of most of your needs when you process lists and arrays. There are some drawbacks, though. The functions process every element in the collection, and sometimes they don't *quite* fit as a solution to the problem, so the higher-order function you provide is difficult to express.

Recursion is the answer to these annoying issues. It lets you process only part of a collection and can also let you express your algorithm more cleanly.

Recursion has a bad reputation for being arcane or confusing. It does take a bit of getting used to, but it's one of those things that—once you start using it—you'll wonder how you ever got along without it. In fact, in this chapter, we'll even use recursion to help us assess the performance of one of the other recursive functions we write. That being said, let's start investigating recursion.

Defining Recursion

You may have seen pictures like this:

It's a drawing of a still life in front of a picture frame. In the picture frame is the still life with a picture frame, which shows the still life with a picture frame, and so on. The image is defined in terms of itself: a drawing of a drawing of a drawing. How far does that sequence go on? In theory, it goes on infinitely. In practice, as soon as the image becomes too small to resolve, the artist stops drawing the smaller images and says, "Okay, that's it."

When dealing with images, this is little more than a clever visual trick. In mathematics and computing, there are many algorithms that can be described compactly in terms of themselves, called *recursive algorithms*. Similarly, functions that call themselves are called *recursive functions*.

Analyzing a Recursive Algorithm

A good example of using recursion is determining whether a word is a palindrome (the same backwards and forwards). Is the word *redivider* a palindrome? To answer this question, you'll probably look at the first and last letter to see if they're the same, then mentally ignore them and look at the remaining part, seeing that the new first and last letter *e*s match, and so on, until you get to the *v* in the middle, and then you'll conclude that the word is a palindrome.

Now this word: *runner*. Again, you can see that the beginning and ending letters are the same, ignore them, and then stop as soon as you see that the *u* and *e* don't match—there's no need to proceed further.

Here's a pseudocode representation of your mental process for finding palindromes:

```
Is this a palindrome?
  If the first and last letters are different, the answer is "no."
  Otherwise, drop the first and last letters. Is this a palindrome?
```

The last step of the pseudocode asks the same question as the first step—there's your recursion. The only problem here is that we have an infinite series of picture frames. There's no way to stop the process. This "how to stop" is called the *base case* in a recursive algorithm. In the case of the palindrome-finding algorithm, we have to stop when we either run out of letters or have only one letter left (since empty strings or a single letter are the same backwards as forwards). Let's update the pseudocode, where the first condition is our base case:

```
Is this a palindrome?
  If there's only one letter or no letters left, the answer is "yes"
  Otherwise:
    If the first and last letters are different, the answer is "no."
    Otherwise, drop the first and last letters. Is this a palindrome?
```

Let's see how this pseudocode works with the word *radar*:

- Does *radar* have one or zero letters? No, it doesn't.
- Are the first and last letters of *radar* different? No, they aren't.
- Drop the first and last letters. Is *ada* a palindrome?
    - Does *ada* have one or zero letters? No, it doesn't.
    - Are the first and last letters of *ada* different? No, they aren't.
    - Drop the first and last letters. Is *d* a palindrome?
        - Does *d* have one or zero letters? Yes. We have a palindrome!

Here's our pseudocode at work on the word *runner*:

- Does *runner* have one or zero letters? No, it doesn't.
- Are the first and last letters of *runner* different? No, they aren't.
- Drop the first and last letters. Is *unne* a palindrome?
    - Does *unne* have one or zero letters? No, it doesn't.
    - Are the first and last letters of *unne* different? Yes, they are. This is not a palindrome.

When you're developing recursive functions, always define your base case first. This will help avoid infinite recursion.

Writing Recursive Functions

Let's translate this pseudocode into actual ReasonML code. You use the keyword rec to indicate that a function can be called recursively. Here's the code for determining if a string is a palindrome, plus some tests.

recursion/palindrome/src/Palindrome.re

```
let rec isPalindrome = (s: string) : bool => {
  let len = Js.String.length(s);
  if (len <= 1) {
    true;
  } else if (Js.String.get(s, 0) != Js.String.get(s, len - 1)) {
    false;
  } else {
    isPalindrome(Js.String.slice(~from= 1, ~to_=len - 1, s));
  }
};

Js.log(isPalindrome("civic")); /* output: true */
Js.log(isPalindrome("deed")); /* output: true */
Js.log(isPalindrome("runner")); /* output: false */
```

Wow. There is lots of new stuff here. On line 1, as advertised, we made the function recursive by specifying rec. (If you leave it out, you'll get an error when ReasonML gets to line 8.) This is also the first time we've seen a function that returns a bool, which has two possible values: true or false.

In line 2, we make a call to the length() function in the Js.String module. You can see it documented at bucklescript.github.io/bucklescript/api/Js.String.html

---

ReasonML Documentation

 As ReasonML is a syntax for OCaml/BuckleScript (as described in Appendix 1, Understanding the ReasonML Ecosystem, on page 169), it can use code written in BuckleScript, such as the JavaScript interface functions. The documentation for these functions is written in OCaml syntax, so you'll have to do some mental translation.

The Js.String.get() function in line 5 takes a string and an index number as its arguments and returns the character at that location within the string.

On line 8, we strip off the beginning and ending letters by calling Js.String.slice(), using named parameters. Note that one of the parameters is named to_. The underscore at the end is required because to is a keyword and can't be used as a variable name.

To see the recursion in action, you can add some calls to Js.log:

recursion/palindrome/src/Palindrome.re
```
let rec isPalindromeLogged = (s: string) : bool => {
  let len = Js.String.length(s);
  Js.log("Seeing if '" ++ s ++ "' is a palindrome");
  if (len <= 1) {
    Js.log("Length is " ++ string_of_int(len) ++ " - we have a palindrome");
    true;
  } else if (Js.String.get(s, 0) != Js.String.get(s, len - 1)) {
    Js.log("Mismatch between " ++ Js.String.get(s, 0) ++ " and "
      ++ Js.String.get(s, len - 1) ++ " - not a palindrome");
    false;
  } else {
    isPalindromeLogged(Js.String.slice(~from= 1, ~to_=len - 1, s));
  }
};
```

Here are two calls and their output:

recursion/palindrome/src/Palindrome.re
```
Js.log(isPalindromeLogged("civic"));
Js.log(isPalindromeLogged("cynic"));

Seeing if 'civic' is a palindrome
Seeing if 'ivi' is a palindrome
Seeing if 'v' is a palindrome
```

```
Length is 1 - we have a palindrome
true
Seeing if 'cynic' is a palindrome
Seeing if 'yni' is a palindrome
Mismatch between y and i - not a palindrome
false
```

Interlude: Measuring Performance

You may have noticed this line:

```
Js.String.slice(~from= 1, ~to_= (len - 2), s)
```

and thought, "Holy crapoley. He's allocating a new string every time he does a recursive call. That must be slow as a turtle trudging through molasses." Let's be clear—it's the reallocation that is expensive, not the fact that we're using recursion. A while loop using the same approach would be doing the reallocation as well. So, even though performance of this particular example isn't a major issue and CPU time is cheap, let's find out how long it takes to determine if a string of 50,000 repetitions of the letter a is a palindrome or not (it is). Writing that code is as good an excuse as any to give more examples of recursion.

We can create the test string with the following function, which produces a string with n repetitions of a given string s. It uses reduce() to take an array of integers ranging from 0 to n - 1 and accumulate copies of s:

recursion/palindrome/src/Palindrome.re
```
let repeatWithReduce = (s: string, n: int) : string => {
  Belt.Array.reduce(Belt.Array.range(0, n - 1), "",
    (accumulator: string, _item: int) => { accumulator ++ s });
};
```

This *is* a horribly inefficient function, as it requires building an array of integers with n entries solely so reduce will have something to work on. Since I want many examples of recursion in this chapter, we'll use recursion to solve the problem more elegantly, even though the most efficient way to build the string is to call String.make(50000, 'a'). To see how the recursive solution works, let's say you want to repeat the string "ha" four times. That's...

* the empty string plus 4 repetitions of "ha", which is the same as
* "ha" plus 3 repetitions of "ha", which is the same as
* "haha" plus 2 repetitions of "ha", which is the same as
* "hahaha" plus 1 repetition of "ha", which is the same as
* "hahahaha" plus 0 repetitions of "ha"—and we're finished

Do you see the recursive pattern here? To "repeat a string n times," you add the string to the result, then "repeat a string $n - 1$ times," with zero being the base case. Translating that into ReasonML, we end up with a recursive function that takes the string to be repeated (s), the accumulated result accumulator, and the number of repetitions n:

recursion/palindrome/src/Palindrome.re
```
let rec repeatRec = (s: string, accumulator: string, n: int) : string => {
  switch (n) {
    | 0 => accumulator /* base case; we're finished */
    | _ => repeatRec(s, accumulator ++ s, n - 1)
  };
};
Js.log(repeatRec("ha", "", 4)); /* output: hahahaha */
```

Does it bother you that you have to provide the empty string as a starting value of the accumulator? Would you rather have just two parameters as in the first version that used reduce()? You can do that by wrapping a version of repeatRec() in a two-argument function:

recursion/palindrome/src/Palindrome.re
```
let repeat = (s: string, n: int) => {
  let rec repeatHelper = (accumulator: string, counter: int) : string => {
    switch (counter) {
      | 0 => accumulator /* base case; we're finished */
      | _ => repeatHelper(accumulator ++ s, counter - 1)
    };
  };
  repeatHelper("", n);
};
Js.log(repeat("ha", 4)); /* output: hahahaha */
```

This technique of making the recursive function a "helper" function and wrapping it in a more appealing interface is a very common technique in functional programming. Note that the repeatHelper() function doesn't need to have s as one of its parameters because that value is available within repeatHelper()'s scope.

Now that we can create the 50,000-character string, it's time to see how well or poorly the isPalindrome() function performs by doing 1,000 iterations of the function and getting the average time. The following code uses Js.Date.now() to get the current time, accurate to the millisecond. We could use reduce() to do the iteration, but let's keep using recursion:

```
recursion/palindrome/src/Palindrome.re
let testString = repeat("a", 50000);
let rec repeatTest = (n: int, accumulatedTime: float) : float => {
  switch (n) {
    | 0 => accumulatedTime
    | _ => {
      let startTime = Js.Date.now();
      let _ = isPalindrome(testString);
      let endTime = Js.Date.now();
      repeatTest(n - 1, accumulatedTime +. (endTime -. startTime))
    }
  }
};
let totalTime = repeatTest(1000, 0.0);

Js.log2("Average time in msec:", totalTime /. 1000.0);
```

On an Intel® Core™ i7-4600U CPU at 2.10GHz, average time for an iteration is 0.7 milliseconds. On a cell phone with a 1.9GHz Snapdragon™ 600 processor, the average time is 4.4 milliseconds. That seems to be an enormous amount of time, but remember: this is for a string with a length of 50,000.

You might be thinking, "Great, but I *still* would like to optimize this function." Here's an exercise for you, then. Write a new function isPalindrome2() that has three parameters: the string being tested and two integers (call them start and finish) that are indices into the string. If the characters at the indices are the same, then recursively call with start + 1 and finish - 1. This avoids doing a Js.String.slice() for every recursive call. I'll leave it to you to figure out the base case. You might want to use a nested "helper" function so users of your function can call it as isPalindrome2(stringValue). You can see my solution at the end of file code/recursion/palindrome/src/Palindrome.re

Understanding Tail Recursion

You may have noticed that the logic of the recursion in all the preceding examples has looked a lot like a while loop in most programming languages. This has been intentional. Look back at the examples, and you'll see that the recursive call has always been the very last part of the recursion. Compare these two recursive functions for repeating a string a given number of times:

```
recursion/tailrec/src/Repeat.re
let rec repeatRec = (s: string, accumulator: string, n: int) : string => {
  switch (n) {
    | 0 => accumulator /* base case; we're finished */
    | _ => repeatRec(s, accumulator ++ s, n - 1)
  };
};
```

```
let rec repeatRec2 = (s:string, n:int) : string => {
  switch (n) {
    | 0 => ""
    | n => s ++ repeatRec2(s, n - 1)
  }
};
```

Why would we use the first version with its accumulator rather than the second version, whose logic is: to repeat a string *n* times, add the string to *n - 1* copies of itself?

Look at what happens when we call the first version with the parameters "go", "", and 3:

- n (3) is not zero, so we call repeatRec() with arguments "go", "go" ("" ++ "go"), and 2

- n (2) is not zero, so we call repeatRec() with arguments "go", "gogo" ("go" ++ "go"), and 1

- n (1) is not zero, so we call repeatRec() with arguments "go", "gogogo" ("gogo" ++ "go"), and 0

- n (0) is zero, so we return the accumulator: "gogogo"

What happens in the second version (this time the steps are numbered)?

1. repeatRec2() is called with "go" and 3.

2. n (3) isn't zero, so the result is s ("go") plus whatever repeatRec2(s, n -1) works out to. In this case we can't do the concatenation right away—we have to wait until we figure out repeatRec2("go", 2), so we make that recursive call.

3. n (2) isn't zero, but we can't do the concatenation to s until we evaluate repeatRec2("go", 2 - 1) so we make that recursive call.

4. n (1) isn't zero, but we *still* can't do the concatenation to s until we evaluate repeatRec2("go", 1 - 1), so we make that recursive call.

5. n is finally zero. Now we know what repeatRec2("go", 0) is—"", so we can complete the concatenation from step 4.

6. The result of that concatenation ("go" ++ "") tells us what repeatRec2("go", 1) worked out to, so we can now complete the concatenation from step 3.

7. The result of that concatenation ("go" ++ "go") tells us what repeatRec2("go", 2) worked out to, so we can now complete the concatenation from step 2, and finally concatenate "go" and "gogo" to give the result of "gogogo".

In the second version of the repeat function, the concatenation is the last operation in the function, not the recursive call, so we have to hold off until we get all the way down to the base case, then wind our way back up. "Holding off" means the intermediate results have to be stored somewhere. The mechanism for doing this is called *stack allocation*, and if we have too many repetitions, we'll run out of space to store those intermediate results and get an error called a *stack overflow*.

The first version, on the other hand, carries a running accumulator so that the intermediate results become part of the recursive call—the very last thing the function does. When the recursive call is the very last operation, the function is *tail recursive*. No extra storage space is needed, and ReasonML will optimize the tail recursion into a JavaScript while loop, so the code avoids stack overflow. Take a look at the JavaScript that ReasonML generates, and you'll see the tail recursive call has indeed become a while.

A Philosophical Note

Most books start teaching recursion with a non-tail recursive version of calculating factorials. (The factorial of a number *n* is the product of all positive integers less than or equal to *n*.) While this matches brilliantly well with one of the mathematical definitions of factorials, the business of holding off until the base case and then winding your way back up the chain adds a level of abstraction that makes recursion seem difficult or mysterious. That's why I started with the palindrome function. It's naturally tail recursive: you work your way down to the base case and you're finished. While expressing the algorithm seems more difficult because it uses an accumulator, the tail-recursive process is conceptually simpler, and that's why I waited to introduce non-tail recursion (with its possibility of stack overflow) until this point in the chapter.

Practicing More Recursion

As you saw in the chapter about collections on page 61, the Belt.Array and Belt.List modules provide a keep() function that produces a new collection of only those items which return true when given to a filtering function.

What if we want to keep only the *indices* of the matching items? For example, when filtering this array for words less than 6 characters long: [| "cow", "aardvark", "squirrel", "fish", "snake", "capybara"|], the result would be [|0, 3, 4|].

Here's the pseudocode, given an empty array of integers as the accumulated result, a position starting at index number zero, and a predicate function f():

```
If the position is at the end of the array:
  return the accumulated result (base case)
otherwise:
  If f(item at current position) returns true:
    Do a recursive call with position appended to the result
    and (position + 1) as the index
  otherwise:
    Do a recursive call with the current result unchanged
    and (position + 1) as the index
```

Here's the recursive function in ReasonML:

```
recursion/keep-indices/src/WithoutHelper.re
let rec keepIndices = (arr: array('a), position: int, accumulator: array(int),
  f : ('a => bool)) : array(int) => {
    if (position < Belt.Array.length(arr)) {
      f(Belt.Array.getUnsafe(arr, position))
        ? keepIndices(arr, position + 1,
            Belt.Array.concat(accumulator, [|position|]), f)
        : keepIndices(arr, position + 1, accumulator, f)
    } else {
      accumulator
    }
};

let words = [|"cow", "aardvark", "squirrel", "fish", "snake", "capybara"|];
let isShortWord = (s: string) : bool => {Js.String.length(s) < 6};
let result = keepIndices(words, 0, [||], isShortWord);
Js.log(result); /* result array: [|0, 3, 4|] */
```

This code would definitely be easier for others to use if it didn't need all those parameters to keepIndices(), so we'll embed it as a helper function:

```
recursion/keep-indices/src/WithHelper.re
let keepIndices = (arr: array('a), f : ('a => bool)) :
  array(int) => {
    let rec helper = (position: int, accumulator: array(int)) : array(int) => {
      if (position < Belt.Array.length(arr)) {
        f(Belt.Array.getUnsafe(arr, position))
          ? helper(position + 1, Belt.Array.concat(accumulator, [|position|]))
          : helper(position + 1, accumulator)
      } else {
        accumulator
      }
    };
    helper(0, [| |]);
};
```

```
let words = [|"cow", "aardvark", "squirrel", "fish", "snake", "capybara"|];
let isShortWord = (s: string) : bool => {Js.String.length(s) < 6};
let result = keepIndices(words, isShortWord);
Js.log(result); /* result array: [|0, 3, 4|] */
```

Using Recursion with Lists

Lists are designed to work hand-in-glove with recursion. Here's a recursive function that will produce the sum of all the numbers in a list up to but not including the first negative number. (Again, you could do this with reduce(), but it would require going through every item in the list.) There are two cases when recursion has to stop: when you encounter a negative number, and when you have an empty list. The latter case happens if there are no negative numbers in the list:

recursion/sum-until-negative/src/Sum.re
```
let rec sumUntilNegative = (items: list(int), total: int) : int => {
  switch (items) {
    | [] => total
    | [x, ..._] when x < 0 => total
    | [x, ...xs] => sumUntilNegative(xs, total + x)
  }
};
```

Let's look at the three cases of the switch statement.

- [] is the empty list.

- [x, ..._] *destructures* the list. The first item in the list is bound to variable x, and the rest of the list (symbolized by ...) is ignored by the underscore. The when clause tests to see if x is negative.

- [x, ...xs] is another destructuring. The first item in the list is bound to x, and the rest of the list is bound to xs (pronounced "ex-es", the plural of "x"). That becomes the new list for sumUntilNegative() to process, with total + x being the new running total. The use of xs is by convention; you can use any name you like, such as remainder or theRest.

This destructuring pattern that assigns the head (first element) and tail (everything else) is very common when dealing with lists.

Here's how we can use recursion to solve the problem of the extra comma and space at the end of our stringOfList() function from Interlude: Displaying Lists, on page 73. The following recursive function distinguishes between lists with zero or one element (the base cases)—where we don't add the comma and space—and lists with more than one element, where we do.

For Lists Only!

 You can't destructure arrays in this way. The internal representation of a list makes getting the tail of a list a very fast operation that doesn't require copying any data. The internal representation of arrays, however, would require copying data to get the tail. This might be acceptable for a small array, but ReasonML has to handle the general case where an array might have hundreds of thousands of elements, each of which takes up a great deal of memory. The performance penalty would be too high, so ReasonML doesn't allow it.

recursion/display-list/src/DisplayList.re
```
let items = [10, 11, 12, 13, 14, 15];
let floatItems = [3.6, 7.9, 8.25, 41.0];

let stringOfList = (items: list('a), stringify: ('a) => string) : string => {
  let rec helper = (accumulator: string, theList: list('a)) => {
    switch (theList) {
      | [] => accumulator
      | [x] => accumulator ++ stringify(x)
      | [x, ...xs] => helper(accumulator ++ stringify(x) ++ ", ", xs)
    }
  };
  helper("[", items) ++ "]";
};

Js.log(stringOfList(items, string_of_int));
Js.log(stringOfList(floatItems, string_of_float));
```

It's Your Turn

The Belt.List module has two functions: take(), which gives you the first *n* elements of a list, and drop(), which gives you everything except the first *n* elements of a list.

Your task is to use recursion to write two new functions, takeWhile() and dropWhile(). Instead of taking a parameter n, the parameter is a predicate function returning true or false when given an item from the list. takeWhile() gives the first elements of the list that satisfy the predicate, stopping when it encounters an element that doesn't fit. dropWhile() returns everything except the first elements of the list that satisfy the predicate. Here is an example:

```
let data = [2, 6, 42, 5, 7, 20, 3];
let isEven = (n) => { (n mod 2) == 0 };

let taken = takeWhile(data, isEven); /* [2, 6, 42] */
let dropped = dropWhile(data, isEven); /* [5, 7, 20, 3] */
```

Both functions stop taking (or dropping) as soon as they encounter an item that doesn't fulfill the predicate. Even though 20 is an even number, it isn't included in the result of the takeWhile().

Hint: You'll probably end up writing nested helper functions for both of these. The Belt.List.reverse() may come in handy for takeWhile().

Summing Up

Recursion, the ability of a function to call itself, lets you take finer control over processing collections. You don't have to process every item, and the code can in some cases be more concise than using map() or reduce(). Most operations where you would use a loop in other languages are done via recursion in ReasonML. When you use recursion, you should make your functions tail recursive if at all possible so that ReasonML can optimize the code it generates. The ability to think recursively is a great skill to add to your programmer's toolkit.

In the next chapter, we'll return to the world of data types. We'll investigate records in ReasonML, which let you make a data structure that contains multiple data types. Additionally, we'll talk about creating your own modules in ReasonML.

CHAPTER 7

Structuring Data with Records and Modules

While the tuple we built in Chapter 5, Using Collections, on page 61 was useful and appropriate for the task, tuples aren't the answer when we have to work with more complex data structures. Instead, ReasonML has *records*, which let you create immutable data structures with field names. This makes your code more organized and readable.

Modules also help in keeping code organized. You'll see that you can create modules to hold data types, records, and functions that operate on them. Modules are also first-class citizens in the ReasonML world. You'll see this in action as we create custom modules that serve as arguments to other modules.

Specifying Records

Tuples were adequate for defining a data type for an order of shirts expressed as the quantity of shirts and the shirt size, as we saw on page 63. But there's more to shirts than just their size. You need to know whether each one is long-sleeved or short-sleeved, the color, pattern, type of cuff, and type of collar. This is definitely not a job for a tuple. There are seven pieces of data, and I'll bet if you walk away from this book for five minutes, you won't remember what order they are in.

First, let's define some data types for size, sleeve length, color, pattern, cuff, and collar:

```
records/shirts/src/Shirts.re
type size =
  | XSmall(int)
  | Small
  | Medium
  | Large
  | XLarge(int);
```

```reason
type sleeve =
  | Short
  | Long
  | XLong; /* for tall people */

type color =
  | White
  | Blue
  | Red
  | Green
  | Brown;

type pattern =
  | Solid
  | Pinstripe
  | Check;

type cuff =
  | Button
  | French
  | NoCuff;

type collar =
  | Button
  | Straight
  | Spread;
```

Even though Button appears in both cuff and collar, there's no conflict. If you have code like this:

```reason
let ambiguous = Button;
let explicit: cuff = Button;
```

In the first line, ReasonML's type inference will choose the last Button you specified (from collar). You can always explicitly tell ReasonML which Button you want by annotating your variables.

Now, we define a record type that gives all the information needed to specify a shirt. It's okay to have a field name the same as its data type. (And yes, short-sleeve shirts with French cuffs really exist.)

records/shirts/src/Shirts.re
```reason
type order = {
  quantity: int,
  size: size,
  sleeve: sleeve,
  color: color,
  pattern: pattern,
  cuff: cuff,
  collar: collar
};
```

Accessing and Updating Records

Here's a definition of a record of the order type and an example of how you access the individual fields using dot notation. You don't have to specify the fields in the same order that you used when you created the data type:

```
records/shirts/src/Shirts.re
let myOrder = {
  quantity: 1,
  size: XLarge(1),
  sleeve: Long,
  color: Blue,
  pattern: Solid,
  cuff: Button,
  collar: Button
};

Js.log2("Size:", myOrder.size); /* Size: [1, tag: 1] */
```

This *looks* a lot like a JavaScript object, but it isn't one. Let me say that again: ReasonML records are *not* JavaScript objects. We'll discuss that when we talk about Interoperating with Objects, on page 123. One of the biggest differences is that records are immutable. You can't change the value of a field in a record. Instead, you have to create a brand-new record. Looking at all those fields, you might be terribly disheartened, but don't worry. ReasonML has the *spread* operator. Here's the code to create a new order the same size as the first one, but with a different color and different style of cuff:

```
records/shirts/src/Shirts.re
let otherOrder = {
  ...myOrder,

  color: White,
  cuff: French
};

Js.log2("Cuff:", otherOrder.cuff); /* Cuff: 1 */
```

Creating Modules

Just as there's not a lot to defining records, there's not much to the basics of modules. In fact, we've been working with modules all along—any .re file is automatically a module, as we saw on page 61 when we put the shirt size data type and its associated functions in a separate file. You can also create a module within a file by using the keyword module, the module name (which *must* begin with a capital letter), an equal sign, and then code in braces. Anything you could put in a ReasonML file can be in a module definition.

If You Really Need Mutability

Okay, maybe records aren't *that* immutable. If you absolutely, positively must have a modifiable field in a record, precede its name with the keyword mutable. As you adopt a more functional programming style, you'll find that you won't need mutability as much as you thought, so try to keep mutable to a minimum.

```
records/mutable-record/src/Demo.re
type person = {
  name: string,
  mutable age: int
};

let happyBirthday = (someone:person) : unit => {
  someone.age = someone.age + 1;
  ()
};

let friend = {
  name: "Juanita Fulano",
  age: 34
};

happyBirthday(friend);
Js.log(friend.age); /* 35 */
```

So let's expand our type definitions and add utility functions for converting to and from strings in our types, each of which will be in its own mini-module. First, let's look at the Size module:

```
records/mod-shirts/src/Shirts.re
module Size = {
  type t =
    | XSmall(int)
    | Small
    | Medium
    | Large
    | XLarge(int);

  let toString = (size: t) : string => {
    switch (size) {
      | XSmall(n) => String.make(n, 'X') ++ "S"
      | Small => "S"
      | Medium => "M"
      | Large => "L"
      | XLarge(n) => String.make(n, 'X') ++ "L"
    }
  };
```

```
  let fromString = (str: string) : option(t) => {
    switch (Js.String.toUpperCase(str)) {
      | "S" => Some(Small)
      | "M" => Some(Medium)
      | "L" => Some(Large)
      | s when Js.Re.test(s, [%re "/^X+S$/"]) =>
          Some(XSmall(String.length(s) - 1))
      | s when Js.Re.test(s, [%re "/^X+L$/"]) =>
          Some(XLarge(String.length(s) - 1));
      | _ => None
    }
  };
};
```

There's something new in the switch statement in fromString(): *guards*. A guard starts with the keyword when, followed by a boolean expression. If the boolean comes out true, that pattern matches. Here's one of the guards:

```
| s when Js.Re.test(s, [%re "/^X+S$/"]) =>
    Some(XSmall(String.length(s) - 1))
```

ReasonML will use this switch case when string s matches the regular expression (one or more occurrences of the letter X followed by the letter S). That regular expression matches strings like XS, XXS, and so forth. The action we take in that case is to figure out how many Xs there are—one less than the length of the string—and use that in the XSmall constructor.

Here's the Cuff module. The definitions of Color, Pattern, Sleeve, and Collar follow the same pattern as Cuff and would be needlessly repetitive here. The full code is in code/records/mod-shirts/src/Shirts.re:

records/mod-shirts/src/Shirts.re
```
module Cuff = {
  type t =
    | Button
    | French
    | NoCuff

  let toString = (cuff: t) : string => {
    switch (cuff) {
      | Button => "button"
      | French => "french"
      | NoCuff => "none"
    }
  };
```

```
let fromString = (s: string) : option(t) => {
  switch (Js.String.toLowerCase(s)) {
  | "button" => Some(Button)
  | "french" => Some(French)
  | ""
  | "none"
  | "nocuff" => Some(NoCuff)
  | _ => None
  }
};
};
```

Multiple Switch Cases

In the Cuff.fromString() function, we've used another feature of the switch statement. If you have multiple patterns that all take the same action, you can list them one after another (on one line or, as we did, on separate lines for readability) and put the action on the last pattern.

So what does using module buy us? First, we have everything in one file instead of multiple files. Second, each module is its own namespace, so we can use a consistent naming system (toString() and fromString()) without fear of name collisions.

Redefining the types requires us to redefine the record type:

records/mod-shirts/src/Shirts.re
```
type order = {
  quantity: int,
  size: Size.t,
  sleeve: Sleeve.t,
  color: Color.t,
  pattern: Pattern.t,
  cuff: Cuff.t,
  collar: Collar.t
};
```

Creating Interface Files for Modules

You don't have to do anything special to let others use your modules. As long as the compiler can find the .re file, you're good to go, and other people can use everything in your modules. However, you might want to have certain private functions or types that aren't available to people using your modules. You can accomplish this by creating *interface files*.

Interface files, which end with .rei, specify function names and types without the function bodies, so the annotation looks like the alternate annotation

Using Nested Modules

In this chapter, I'm duplicating the code for the type-defining modules used in the shirt examples because I want each example to be independent of the others. If we were writing an application where several files needed to use the shirt types, we'd move them to a file named, say, Shirt.re. Then, in a file named, say, Order.re, we could write code like this:

```
let price = switch (order.sleeve) {
  | Shirt.Sleeve.Short => 12.00
  | Shirt.Sleeve.Long => 15.00
  | Shirt.Sleeve.XLong => 16.00
};
```

You can also directly nest modules:

records/books/src/BookExample.re
```
module Book = {
  module Author = {
    type t = {
      firstName: string,
      lastName: string,
    };
  };

  type t = {
    title: string,
    author: Author.t,
    isbn13: string
  };
};

let b: Book.t = {
  title: "Anathem",
  author: {
      firstName: "Neal",
      lastName: "Stephenson"
  },
  isbn13: "978-0-06-147409-5"
};

Js.log(b.author.lastName); /* Stephenson */
```

style we examined on page 23, with no equal sign after the function name and the return type after the =>. These .rei files are useful for documentation. Much like header files in a language like C or C++, they give other people a convenient list of functions available in a module. *Only* the functions listed in the .rei file are available to people using your module, so this gives you the ability to create private functions.

We could create the interface files by hand, but it's easier to compile the project first. Then we can use the BuckleScript compiler's -bs-re-out option to analyze its intermediate output files and create the .rei file. This avoids a lot of repetitive busy work on our part. The name of the intermediate output file is the name of your source file, dropping the .re and adding a hyphen, the camel case name of your project, and .cmi.

Here's the command to create the interface file for Shirts.re:

```
bsc -bs-re-out lib/bs/src/Shirts-ModShirts.cmi  > src/Shirts.rei
```

This is what part of that output file looks like:

records/mod-shirts/src/Shirts.rei
```
module Size:
  {
    type t = XSmall(int) | Small | Medium | Large | XLarge(int);
    let toString: t => string;
    let fromString: string => option(t);
  };
module Sleeve:
  {
    type t = Short | Long | XLong;
    let toString: t => string;
    let fromString: string => option(t);
  };
module Color:
  {
    type t = White | Blue | Red | Green | Brown;
    let toString: t => string;
    let fromString: string => option(t);
  };
```

Putting Modules to Work

Now that we have our records and modules set up, we're going to write a command-line NodeJS program in ReasonML that reads a file of shirt orders, with each order represented as a line of comma-separated values. The program will get the name of the file to read from the command line argument and output a list of sales by size, color, pattern, collar, and cuff type. Here's what it looks like when it grows up:

```
$ node src/Stats.bs.js orders.csv
Color Quantity
white 118
blue 114
red 73
...
```

Here are the first few lines of a sample input file, with the first line being a header line:

```
Quantity,Size,Color,Pattern,Collar,Sleeve,Cuff
6,L,white,solid,straight,long,button
5,L,blue,pinstripe,straight,xlong,button
5,M,red,check,spread,long,button
4,M,blue,check,button,xlong,french
```

You can see a file containing 100 orders at code/records/shirt-stats/orders.csv and a smaller test file of six orders at code/records/shirt-stats/mini-orders.csv.

Accessing Command Line Arguments

BuckleScript has a Node module that provides an interface to NodeJs. According to the website, "it is still a work in progress, use it with care, and we may break API backward compatibility in the future."[1] I'm willing to let the future take care of itself, so here is the code you need to get a file name from the command line.

```
records/shirt-stats/src/Stats.re
let nodeArg = Belt.Array.get(Node.Process.argv, 0);
let progArg = Belt.Array.get(Node.Process.argv, 1);
let fileArg = Belt.Array.get(Node.Process.argv, 2);

switch (nodeArg, progArg, fileArg) {
  | (_, _, Some(inFileName)) => processFile(inFileName)
  | (Some(node), Some(prog), _) =>
    Js.log("Usage: " ++ node ++ " " ++ prog ++ " inputfile.csv")
  | (_, _, _) =>
    Js.log("How did you get here without NodeJS or a program to run?")
};
```

This code gets the first three elements of the Node.process.argv array: the path to the NodeJS executable, the name of the file being executed, and any other command-line arguments you may have provided. The Belt.Array.get() returns an option value. When we have a file argument (argv[2]), we process that file. Otherwise, we print an error message explaining how the program is used. The last case in the switch statement handles the "can't happen" case when we have neither a path to NodeJS nor our program.

Processing the File

To process the file, we read in the entire file into a single string, split it on newlines, discard the header line, use reduce() to convert each line to an order, and—if the conversion is successful—add it to a list. Once that list is complete,

---

1. bucklescript.github.io/bucklescript/api/index.html

we hand it to a function that prints the statistics. The return value from the processFile() function is unit. We don't expect it to return anything we need anywhere else—we only want it for its side effects of reading a file and printing results.

```
records/shirt-stats/src/Stats.re
let processFile = (inFileName: string): unit => {
  let fileContents = Node.Fs.readFileAsUtf8Sync(inFileName);
  let lines = Js.String.split("\n", fileContents) ->
    Belt.Array.sliceToEnd(1); /* get rid of header line */

  let orders = Belt.Array.reduce(lines, [], lineReducer);

  printStatistics(orders);
};
```

Creating a Record

Here's the plan for the lineReducer() function that adds a record from a line in the CSV file to the accumulator. This is where, as reviewer António Monteiro put it, we're "hitting the problem that strongly typed languages have, which is boundaries between the internal typing and external data." This part is tricky, so I'll go through my thought process. Those of you who are experienced with functional programming can skim to the end of this subsection.

The first steps are relatively straightforward: split the line on commas, creating an array of strings. If the number of items in the array doesn't equal the number of expected items, then I have bad data and return the accumulator unchanged.

If I *do* have the correct number of items, there's no guarantee that they all contain valid data. This is a job for an option(order). The plan is to start with an initialized Some(order) and look at the first item in the array (the quantity). If it's a valid integer, I'll update my Some(order). If not, the result is None.

If I still have a valid order, I try converting the second string in the array to a Size. If successful, I update the order. If not, it's None, and so on. My first version of the plan looked like this, where initial is my starting value:

```
let result1 =  switch (optInt(items[0])) {
    | Some(n) => Some({...initial, quantity: n})
    | None => None;
};

let result2 = switch (result1) {
  | Some(r) => switch (Size.fromString(items[1])) {
    | Some(sz) => Some({...r, size: sz}})
    | None => None;
  }
  | None => None;
};
```

```
let result3 = switch(result2) {
  | Some(r) => switch (Color.fromString(items[2])) {
      | Some(c) => Some({...r, color: c}})
      | None => None
    }
  | None => None
};

/* etc. */
```

There's nothing inherently wrong with this code. It does exactly what I want, and I could have used it as-is. However. I didn't like all those switches, Somes, and Nones. This code looks like what we saw at the beginning of the discussion of option on page 41. There, we used map() and flatMap() to shorten a similar series of switches. That's what I want to do here, but I can't use either of those functions. They're designed for functions with one argument, and here I have *two* option variables: the order I'm building, and the result from the fromString() call.

There is no Belt.Option.map2(), but there's no law that says I can't write my own:

records/shirt-stats/src/Stats.re
```
let map2 = (optX, optY, f) =>
  switch (optX, optY) {
  | (Some(x), Some(y)) => Some(f(x, y))
  | (_, _) => None
  };
```

In map2(), optX and optY are option arguments, and f is a function that takes two non-option arguments and returns a non-option value. If both optX and optY are Some(), it's okay to apply function f() to their contents and wrap up the result in Some(). Otherwise, one or both of them must be None, and the result will be None. Once I have map2(), I can write my reducer function:

records/shirt-stats/src/Stats.re
```
Line 1  let lineReducer = (acc: list(order), line: string): list(order) => {
          let items = Js.String.split(",", line);
          if (Belt.Array.length(items) != 7) {
            acc;
     5    } else {
            let initial =
              Some({
                quantity: 0,
                size: Small,
    10          sleeve: Short,
                color: White,
                pattern: Solid,
                cuff: Button,
                collar: Straight,
    15        });
```

```
     let orderRecord = map2(initial, optInt(items[0]),
         (result, n) => {...result, quantity: n})
       -> map2(Size.fromString(items[1]),
         (result, sz) => {...result, size: sz})
       -> map2(Color.fromString(items[2]),
         (result, c) => {... result, color: c})
       -> map2(Pattern.fromString(items[3]),
         (result, pat) => {...result, pattern: pat})
       -> map2(Collar.fromString(items[4]),
         (result, coll) => {...result, collar: coll})
       -> map2(Sleeve.fromString(items[5]),
         (result, sleeve) => {...result, sleeve: sleeve})
       -> map2(Cuff.fromString(items[6]),
         (result, cuff) => {...result, cuff: cuff});

     switch (orderRecord) {
       | Some(result) => [result, ...acc]
       | None => acc
     };
   };
 };
```

In line 7, I put a Some() around my initial order so that I could use map2() everywhere. I use an anonymous function to update the order, as in lines 18 and 20, and I'll use a pipe first to pass the result of each map2() to the next one in line.

Once I finish analyzing the strings in the array (line 32), I either have a valid order, which I add to the accumulated list, or I have None and leave the accumulated list unchanged.

Again, this was *my* thought process. You might prefer the original long way I wrote the code, or you may have gone directly to the map2 solution, or you may have even figured out a different, better way of doing it.

Analyzing the Data

Now that we have a list of orders, we can analyze it. The first thing we'll do is get a distribution by color, and we'll need a new sort of collection to do this efficiently. Instead of an array, which is indexed by number, we'd like a key-and-value collection where the key is a Color.t variant and the value is the number of shirts of that color. A key/value collection is called a *dictionary* in Python and *hash*, *hash table*, or *associative array* in other languages. In ReasonML, it's called ... a Map. Yes, I know. Yet another use of the word "map" for a completely different purpose.

There are several different implementations of key/value in ReasonML; the List module implements it as a list of (key, value) tuples. This has the advantage of simplicity, but is not particularly speedy, as most operations require you to traverse the list. The Map module from the OCaml standard library is a better choice, as it is optimized for the task. The best choice, and the one we'll use here, is the Belt.Map module.

Belt.Map provides three pre-built types of maps: Belt.Map.Int, where the keys are integers, Belt.Map.String, where the keys are strings, and Belt.Map.Dict, which is labeled "for advanced use only." In our case, the key is a Color.t, not an integer or string, so we have to use the generic Belt.Map. In order to do its job efficiently, Belt.Map needs to be able to compare the keys of items in the map. This requires us to provide a *comparator* module when creating a map. Here's the comparator that will tell Belt.Map how to compare Color.t values:

```
records/shirt-stats/src/Stats.re
Line 1  module ColorComparator =
     2    Belt.Id.MakeComparable({
     3      type t = Color.t;
     4      let cmp = compare;
     5    });
```

Line 3 defines the data type being compared. Line 4 defines a function to be used to compare sizes. In this case, we're using the built-in compare() function. This is a function that compares two items and returns a negative integer if the first item is less than the second, zero if the two items are equal, and a positive integer if the first item is greater than the second. Here is compare() in action with various Color.t values.

```
Js.log(compare(Color.White, Color.Red));   /* -1 */
Js.log(compare(Color.Green, Color.Green));  /* 0 */
Js.log(compare(Color.Brown, Color.Blue));   /* 1 */
```

The result of Belt.Id.MakeComparable() (called in line 2) is a uniquely identified module that we can give to Belt.Map.make():

Modules Creating Modules

 Just as you can pass functions as arguments to other functions, ReasonML allows you to pass modules as arguments to other modules. A module that takes another module as an argument is called a *functor*. You can see a full explanation of functors online.[2]

---

2. reasonml.github.io/docs/en/module#module-functions-functors

Here's the function for generating the statistics, which also returns unit:

```
records/shirt-stats/src/Stats.re
Line 1  type colorMapType = Belt.Map.t(Color.t, int, ColorComparator.identity);

        let colorReducer = (accumulatedMap: colorMapType, item: order): colorMapType
        => {
     5    let n = Belt.Map.getWithDefault(accumulatedMap, item.color, 0);
          Belt.Map.set(accumulatedMap, item.color, n + item.quantity);
        }

        let printStatistics = (orders: list(order)): unit => {
    10    let colorDistribution =
            Belt.List.reduce(
              orders,
              Belt.Map.make(~id=(module ColorComparator)),
              colorReducer);
    15    Js.log2("Color","Quantity");
          Belt.Map.forEach(colorDistribution,
            (key, value) => Js.log2(Color.toString(key), value)
          );
        };
```

We start off with a type alias in line 1 to allow us to annotate functions in a readable manner.

The printStatistics()() function creates a map (colorDistribution) by reducing the orders list. The initial value of the accumulator is a new, empty map created on line 13. The reducing function on line 3 has the current map as its accumulator and the current item from the order list. It uses Belt.map.getWithDefault() to get the current count associated with a item's color—or zero if it's not in the map yet (line 5), and then creates a new map with the accumulator, setting the value for item.color to its current value plus the quantity ordered (line 6). The result is now a map with the shirt colors as keys and the total number ordered as the values.

Printing the Data

We now have to iterate through the entries in colorDistribution and print them out. This is not a job for Belt.Map.map() or Belt.Map.reduce(), which return some value. We don't need a return value—we just want output. This is why Belt.Map.foreach() exists. Given a key/value map, it iterates through each item in the map (in ascending order of its keys) and calls a function that we provide. Our anonymous function (on line 17) takes a key and value as its parameters and returns unit.

It's Your Turn

Our program currently shows the distribution only for colors. Add the code to show distribution for size, sleeve, pattern, cuff, and collar.

Here are some things to consider:

1. You'll need to implement comparators for all the data types. All of them can use the built-in compare() procedure, but if you try using it with the Size.t type, you will get some interesting results.

```
Js.log(compare(Size.Small, Size.Medium)); /* -1  as expected */
Js.log(compare(Size.XLarge(3), Size.XLarge(2))); /* 1   as expected */
Js.log(compare(Size.Large, Size.XLarge(1))); /* -1 as expected */
Js.log(compare(Size.XSmall(2), Size.Medium)); /* 1 not as expected */
```

Because of the way ReasonML represents variant data types, the last comparison says that XSmall(2) is greater than Medium. That means that Belt.Map.forEach will print the sizes in the "wrong" order. If you're okay with that, use compare. If you prefer to see the keys in their correct order, you'll have to implement a function in the Size module that takes two Size.t items and returns the correct result of comparison. The signature of your function should look like this:

```
let compareSize = (a: t, b: t) : int => {
  /* your code here */
};
```

You can then use Size.compareSize for the cmp in your comparator module.

2. You could copy and paste the code in the printStatistics() function for each of the other fields and then edit the map name, the field accessor in Belt.Map.set(), and the module name preceding the toString() call. That will work fine, but it's repetitive, and the editing process is error-prone. Find a way to create other functions that will minimize the repetitive code. You can see my solution in code/records/stats-complete/src/Stats.re.

Creating the CSV File

 I can assure you that I didn't write each of the 100 lines in code/records/stats-complete/orders.csv by hand. Instead, I wrote a program to generate them for me. That program didn't need any specialized modules or records, so it's not a good example for this chapter. You might, however, want to try your hand at writing a program to generate random orders. As an extra challenge, don't give equal distributions of all the choices—your program should, for example, generate more medium shirts than XXL shirts and more button cuffs than French cuffs. You can see my version in code/records/make-csv/src/MakeCSV.re.

Summing Up

Every ReasonML file is automatically a module, but you are free to define a module within a file at any time. A module within a file can contain anything that you'd put in a ReasonML file—for example, type definitions, function definitions, and even other modules.

ReasonML records are immutable data structures with field names that exist at compile time. You access the fields with the dot operator (.) and update fields (which creates a new record) using the spread operator (...). They look like JavaScript objects, but they aren't.

If you're still pining for JavaScript objects—or, more likely, you need to interoperate with existing JavaScript libraries that are object-based—well, that's what we'll look at in the next chapter.

CHAPTER 8

Connecting to JavaScript

In this chapter, you'll learn how to interoperate with existing JavaScript code by calling functions written in JavaScript and by creating and accessing JavaScript objects. This lets your ReasonML programs make use of the enormous number of libraries and modules written in JavaScript. By the end of this chapter, we'll have developed a program that involves interoperating with JavaScript on both the client and server, using the shirt orders that we looked at in Putting Modules to Work, on page 110.

- We'll set up an Express[1] server and send the client an HTML page with a form.

Size	Total
XS	29
S	63
M	139
L	73
XL	58
XXL	38

- The client will select the information they want summarized and send the server an XHTTP request.

- The server will use Papa Parse,[2] a JavaScript module that parses CSV files, to read in the shirt order data file, create a JSON response, and send it back.

- The client will take the response and create an HTML table displaying the results, as you see in the figure.

To do all this, we'll need to use existing ReasonML bindings to JavaScript packages (for Express and JSON), write our own bindings (for Papa Parse), and interoperate with JavaScript objects. Let's get started.

Adding Raw JavaScript

The easiest and least type-safe way to access JavaScript is by placing raw JavaScript code in the middle of your ReasonML code. The generic form is:

---

1.   expressjs.com/
2.   www.papaparse.com/

[%raw {| /* Js expression */ |}]. The JavaScript must be an *expression*, not a series of statements, nor even an expression followed by a semicolon.

What if you really need multiple statements? You can get around the limitation by using an immediately invoked function expression (IIFE). You create an IIFE by putting the statements into an anonymous JavaScript function and then calling the function with a set of parentheses () at the end.

As an example, here's a program using an IIFE with raw JavaScript to get the current date and time as a string:

```
interop/raw-js/src/RawJS.re
let rightNow = [%raw {|
 function () {
  var d = new Date();
  return d.toString();
 }()
|}];

let message = "It is now " ++ rightNow;
Js.log(message);
```

Using [%raw] is unsatisfying because it puts you back in the JavaScript world, and if you wanted to write in plain JavaScript, you would not be reading this book. However, if you need to interoperate with JavaScript and none of the other techniques we're going to examine work, you have [%raw] as a last resort. The BuckleScript site has more details and cautionary notes about [%raw].[3]

Binding to Existing Functions

There's a more satisfying way to use the functions in the JavaScript Date object: write a *binding* that tells ReasonML how it should communicate with them. Before writing your own bindings, you may want to visit the Reason Package index at redex.github.io to see if the needed bindings already exist. You can also try doing an npm search for bs- as a prefix to the package name whose bindings you want.

Although there's already a set of bindings for Date,[4] it's good for us to derive some of them ourselves so we're ready when we come across a library that doesn't have bindings. Among the things we'll do from ReasonML:

---

3. bucklescript.github.io/docs/en/embed-raw-javascript
4. bucklescript.github.io/bucklescript/api/Js.Date.html

- Create a new Date object.

- Call class-level methods such as now(), which returns the number of milliseconds since January 1, 1970 00:00:00 UTC (the *epoch*), and parse(), which converts a string to milliseconds since the epoch or NaN if the string is invalid.

- Call instance methods such as toString(), which returns a Date object's string representation, and getFullYear(), which returns the four-digit year specified by a given Date object.

The general plan for defining a binding is to give one or more directives that tell what kind of binding we need, the keyword external, the ReasonML name of the binding and its type annotation, and the name of the function in the JavaScript code. Here are our bindings for Date, in a file whose name is JsDate.re:

```
interop/date/src/JsDate.re
type t;
[@bs.new] external createDate: unit => t = "Date";
[@bs.scope "Date"] [@bs.val] external now: unit => float = "";
[@bs.scope "Date"] [@bs.val] external jsDateParse: string => float = "parse";
[@bs.send] external toString: t => string = "",
[@bs.send] external getFullYear: t => float = "";

let parse = (s: string): option(float) => {
  let result = jsDateParse(s);
  if (Js.Float.isNaN(result)) {
    None;
  } else {
    Some(result);
  }
};
```

Line 1 gives a name for ReasonML to use for the Date. Since we're in file JsDate.re, other programs will refer to the JsDate.t type.

Line 2 shows how to call the JavaScript new() from ReasonML. The directive is [@bs.new]. We'll use the name createDate, which takes no arguments (unit) and returns our type (t). Calling createDate() will compile to new Date() in the resulting JavaScript, so we use "Date" as the JavaScript name.

The now() method in line 3 is a class method of Date rather than an instance method, so we need to specify its module using [@bs.scope "Date"], which specifies the class name. The [@bs.val] directive says we're binding to a value. The ReasonML function name is now. It takes no arguments (unit) and returns a float. The name of the JavaScript function is also now, so we can use a shortcut and use the empty string as the JavaScript name.

In line 4, I have made a design decision. I would prefer to have parse() return an option(float) rather than NaN or undefined, so I made up a new name (jsDateParse()) that calls the JavaScript parse() function.

That takes care of the class-level methods. Let's look at an instance method like toString. In JavaScript, we'd write something like this:

```
var d = new Date();
var dateStr = d.toString();
```

Because we aren't using object-orientation, we have to translate the instance method call into the following ReasonML, where the object becomes the first parameter to our function:

```
let d = JsDate.createDate();
let dateStr = JsDate.toString(d);
```

That's the purpose of the [@bs.send] directive in line 5. It tells us that the first parameter in the ReasonML function is the object, and the function name is the method to call on that object. Put in generic terms: [@bs.send] says that a JavaScript call of the form someObject.name(arg1, arg2, ...) is written in ReasonML as name(someObject, arg1, arg2, ...).

The getFullYear() method in line 6 uses the same [@bs.send] directive to indicate that we're calling the instance method getFullYear on a Date object provided as the argument.

Finally, starting in line 8, I write the parse() method that I want users of my module to employ. It calls jsDateParse() and returns an option(float)—Some(result) if the parse succeeded, or None if JavaScript gave me NaN.

Hiding a Binding

If I want to make sure that people using my JsDate bindings can't inadvertently use the jsDateParse() bindings, I can create a .rei file as described on page 108 to control which bindings are exposed:

```
                    interop/date/src/JsDate.rei
type t;
let createDate: (unit) => t;
let now: (unit) => float;
let toString: (t) => string;
let getFullYear: (t) => float;
let parse: (string) => option(float);
```

Interoperating with Data Types

In the preceding examples, you saw a little bit of JavaScript and ReasonML data type interaction. ReasonML shares certain data types with JavaScript.

The ReasonML string, bool, and array types correspond directly to JavaScript string, boolean, and array types. Tuples are compiled to JavaScript arrays, which is very handy if you ever need to process a non-homogeneous array from JavaScript—treat it as a tuple on the ReasonML side. You may depend upon these shared data types. The BuckleScript site has a handy cheat sheet for you.[5]

For all other data types, ReasonML compiles to a JavaScript representation that can vary depending on the version of the compiler. For example, as of this writing, a ReasonML char value compiles to the numeric code point for that character on the JavaScript side, and a ReasonML list compiles to an array of arrays. Don't rely on the internal structures in your JavaScript because they're subject to change. Instead, do conversions to shared data types:

```
let ch = 'a';
let s = String.make(1, ch); /* convert character to string */

let dataList = [1, 2, 3, 4];
let dataArray = Belt.List.toArray(dataList);
let newList = Belt.List.fromArray(dataArray);
```

Interoperating with Objects

Objects are the JavaScript data structure you'll almost certainly be working with the most. As we discussed in the chapter on records and modules on page 105, ReasonML records aren't objects. However, to interoperate with JavaScript objects, we'll use a type definition that looks a lot like that of a record.

Consider this JavaScript object, which describes metadata from Papa Parse, a JavaScript module that parses comma-separated value files:

```
{
  delimiter: // Delimiter used
  linebreak: // Line break sequence used
  aborted:   // Whether process was aborted
  fields:    // Array of field names
  truncated: // Whether preview consumed all input
}
```

We represent this data type as follows. To make the example a bit clearer, we aren't putting this type in its own module:

---

5.   bucklescript.github.io/docs/en/common-data-types#cheat-sheet

interop/record/src/RecordExample.re
```
[@bs.deriving abstract] type meta = {
  delimiter: string,
  linebreak: string,
  aborted: bool,
  fields: array(string),
  truncated: bool
};
```

The [@bs.deriving abstract] tells ReasonML to build functions that let us create meta objects and access them. The function for creating an object has the same name as the type, and its arguments are labeled the same as the fields. Because the arguments are labeled, they can be in any order:

interop/record/src/RecordExample.re
```
let metaData = meta(~delimiter=",",~aborted=false,
  ~linebreak="\n", ~truncated=false,
  ~fields=[|"Quantity", "Size", "Color"|]);
```

The preceding code generates this JavaScript:

```
var metaData = {
  delimiter: ",",
  linebreak: "\n",
  aborted: false,
  fields: /* array */[
    "Quantity",
    "Size",
    "Color"
  ],
  truncated: false
};
```

The [@bs.deriving abstract] directive also creates functions of the form fieldnameGet. These functions take an object as their argument and return the value of the given fieldname:

interop/record/src/RecordExample.re
```
Js.log(fieldsGet(metaData)); /* ["Quantity", "Size", "Color"] */
Js.log(truncatedGet(metaData)); /* false */
```

Let's take a look at the JavaScript object that Papa Parse returns for an error:

```
{
  type: "",      // A generalization of the error
  code: "",      // Standardized error code
  message: "",   // Human-readable details
  row: 0,        // Row index of parsed data where error is
}
```

Handling Missing Fields

 Since JavaScript is dynamic, you can't count on a library returning an object with all the fields you've specified in the ReasonML type. For example, in Papa Parse, if you haven't specified a header row in the CSV you're parsing, the meta object won't have the field named fields, and calling fieldsGet() will return undefined. You can test for this situation by using the Js.Nullable.isNullable() function, which returns true if the value passed to it is null or undefined.

There's a potential problem here: the field name type is a reserved word in ReasonML, so we can't use it in our type definition. To solve this problem, ReasonML lets us use @bs.as to specify a non-reserved name such as type_ (the convention is to add a trailing underscore) that will generate type in the JavaScript.

interop/record/src/RecordExample.re
```
[@bs.deriving abstract] type error = {
  [@bs.as "type"]  type_: string,
  code: string,
  message: string,
  row: int,
  index: int
};

let errExample = error(~code="InvalidQuotes",
  ~type_="Quotes", ~row=1, ~index=30,
  ~message="Trailing quote on quoted field is malformed");
```

And here is the JavaScript:

```
var errExample = {
  type: "Quotes",
  code: "InvalidQuotes",
  message: "Trailing quote on quoted field is malformed",
  row: 1,
  index: 30
};
```

It's Your Turn

Add record types and bindings to the code that analyzes shirt orders as described on page 116, to allow it to use Papa Parse. Start with file code/interop/stats/src/Stats.re, which contains comments that tell you what you need to add. Look for sections marked TODO: for instructions. The Error module, which we've already developed, is in the file as a guide for the other records you need to create. I've taken the shirt-oriented types and separated them into file code/interop/stats/src/Shirt.re to reduce the size of the Stats.re file.

You'll need to do npm install --save papaparse in the stats directory to run the code:

```
# presume you are in the stats directory
bsb -make-world
node src/Stats.bs.js orders.csv
```

You may see the solution in code/interop/stats-complete/src/Stats.re.

Working with JSON

JSON (JavaScript Object Notation) is the last piece of the puzzle we'll need to solve in order to write our project for this chapter. We need JSON to send the server data to the client in a way that it can understand, and the client has to be able to decode the JSON object into ReasonML data types.

There are two main JSON libraries for ReasonML: bs-json[6] and bs-decode.[7] The main differences are:

- bs-json can be used in a way that throws exceptions when it finds bad JSON, whereas bs-decode always returns an option or Belt.Result when it encounters errors.

- bs-json has facilities for parsing and encoding JSON, whereas bs-decode devotes itself purely to decoding, as its name indicates.

In this section, we'll go with bs-json, and create a project named json-example. We'll add bs-json to the dependencies in bsconfig.json:

```
"bs-dependencies": [
   "@glennsl/bs-json"
],
```

Then we npm install --save @glennsl/bs-json. Once that's set up, you're ready to parse a JSON string. You can use the parse() function, which returns an option(Json.t) result, or you can use parseOrRaise(), which, if successful, returns a Json.t result, or raises a ParseError exception in the case of an error.

Decoding JSON

Once you have a JSON object (Json.t), you can decode the JSON object into ReasonML data types.

---

6.   github.com/glennsl/bs-json
7.   github.com/mlms13/bs-decode

interop/json-example/src/JsonExample.re

```
Line 1  module D = Json.Decode;

        let decodedStr = switch (Json.parse({js|"two words"|js})) {
          | Some(jsonStr) => D.string(jsonStr)
     5    | None => "";
        };
        Js.log(decodedStr); /* "two words" */

        /* Compose array decoder with float decoder with partial application */
    10  let floatArrayDecoder = D.array(D.float);
        let decodedArray =
          Json.parse("[3.4, 5.6, 7.8]")
          -> Belt.Option.mapWithDefault([||], floatArrayDecoder);
        Js.log(decodedArray); /* [|3.4, 5.6, 7.8|] */
    15
        let decodedObj = switch (Json.parse({|{"size": "XXL", "qty": 10}|})) {
          | Some(jsonObj) => D.field("qty", D.int, jsonObj)
          | None => 0;
        };
    20  Js.log(decodedObj); /* 10 */
```

To make our lives easier, let's use D as an abbreviation for the Json.Decode module in line 1. Line 4 shows the conversion of a JSON string to a ReasonML string.

To convert a JSON array to a ReasonML array, you need to tell the decoder the array elements' type, as in line 10. In this code, we've gotten fancy and built a decoder by composing two functions. We're also using Belt.Option.map-WithDefault() to avoid the need for a switch.

Finally, you can extract fields from a JSON object, as in line 17, by specifying the field name, its type, and the JSON object.

For a more complete example, here's code that will convert a JSON object to a ReasonML record:

interop/json-example/src/JsonExample.re

```
type statsRecord = {
  title: string,
  choices: array(string),
  totals: array(int)
};

let objStats = {js|{"title": "color",
  "choices": ["White", "Blue", "Red", "Green", "Brown"],
  "totals": [118, 114, 73, 67,28]}
|js};
```

```
let colorStats = switch (Json.parse(objStats)) {
  | Some(jsonObj) =>
      {
        title: D.field("title", D.string, jsonObj),
        choices: D.field("choices", D.array(D.string), jsonObj),
        totals: D.field("totals", D.array(D.int), jsonObj)
      }
  | None => { title: "", choices: [| |], totals: [| |] }
};
Js.log(colorStats)
```

Encoding JSON

If you're interoperating with a JavaScript library that expects you to send it a JSON object, you'll need to encode your ReasonML data as JSON:

interop/json-example/src/JsonExample.re

```
Line 1  let sleeveStats = {
    -     title: "sleeve",
    -     choices: [|"short sleeve", "long sleeve", "extra-long sleeve"|],
    -     totals: [| 129, 217, 54 |]
    5   };
    -
    -   module E = Json.Encode;
    -
    -   let sleeveJson = E.object_([
   10     ("title", E.string(sleeveStats.title)),
    -     ("choices", E.stringArray(sleeveStats.choices)),
    -     ("totals", E.array(E.int, sleeveStats.totals))]);
    -
    -   Js.log(Json.stringify(sleeveJson));
```

As with decoding, we make a module alias in line 7. To create a JSON object, we use Json.Encode.object_(), starting in line 9. The trailing underscore is necessary to avoid a collision with the ReasonML object keyword. The object_() function takes a list of tuples as its argument. The first element of the tuple is the field name, and the second is its encoded value. For ReasonML data types that have direct equivalents in JavaScript, there are specialized encoder functions, such as string() and stringArray() in lines 10 and 11. There's a specialized numArray() encoder, but it requires an array of float, and we have an array of integer in line 4. We can solve this problem by using the generic array() encoder. Its first argument is a function that encodes the element type in the array (int), and the second argument is the array to be encoded (line 12).

The result is a JSON object suitable for passing to a function that expects an object. If you need to convert the JSON object to a string, use the Json.stringify() function as in line 14.

Setting Up the Server

We now have all the parts we need for our project. Let's set up the server. But first, a disclaimer: this section isn't intended as a complete guide to using Express. It provides just enough explanation to get our project working.

Create a project named server, install the Express server, and add the dependencies to the bsconfig.json file:

```
cd server
npm install --save express # the server
npm install --save bs-express # ReasonML bindings
npm install --save @glennsl/bs-json
npm install --save papaparse # to parse the CSV file

"bs-dependencies": [
    "bs-express",
    "@glennsl/bs-json"
],
```

The server code starts by instantiating a server and then telling it to listen on port 3000:

```
interop/server/src/Server.re
let onListen = e =>
  switch (e) {
  | exception (Js.Exn.Error(e)) =>
    Js.log(e);
    Node.Process.exit(1);
  | _ => Js.log("Listening at http://127.0.0.1:3000")
  };

let app = Express.express();
let server = Express.App.listen(app, ~port=3000, ~onListen, ());
```

The listen() function specifies the application, the port, and a callback function that's invoked when the connection is made or if there's an error. The () at the end of the call is required because listen has default labeled parameters, as described in Providing Default Values for Labeled Parameters, on page 19.

This code is followed by a series of *routes* that tell the server how to respond to GET or POST requests using these functions, all of which are part of the Express module:

App.get() and App.post() These functions have three parameters: the server app, the route path, and a function to handle the request. If you precede a part of the path with a colon, it becomes a route parameter that you can access in your handler.

Middleware.from() This function takes a handler function as its parameter. The function you give to Middleware.from() has two parameters: the next handler in a chain, and the request that the server received.

Request.query() This function takes a request as its single parameter and returns a Js.Dict.t(Js.Json.t) object like {"key":"value"} containing information about the request query string (the part after the ? in the URL).

Response.sendFile() This function has two parameters: a URL and an object containing options, such as the root directory for relative file names and HTTP headers to serve with the file.

Response.sendStatus() This function has one parameter: the status code to send to the client. The code has data type Response.StatusCode.t.

Response.sendJson() This function has one parameter: a JSON object to send to the client. It sends a string that represents the object.

The first route is for the root path (/). It serves up file index.html.

```
interop/server/src/Server.re
[@bs.deriving abstract]
type options = {
  root: string,
};

Express.App.get(app, ~path="/",
  Express.Middleware.from((_, _) => {
    Express.Response.sendFile("index.html", options(~root="./dist"));
  }
));
```

We will create a JavaScript object for the sendFile() options parameter. In this case, the root option tells the server that relative path names should be served from the dist directory. This code is using a relative path name for the root—in a production environment, you would be well advised to use an absolute path name.

Testing the Server

This is a perfect time to test the code we have so far. Create a directory named dist and put an index.html file in it, with some minimal content:

```
<!DOCTYPE html>
<html>
  <head>
    <title>Test File</title>
  </head>
```

```
<body>
  <h1>It works!</h1>
</body>
</html>
```

Build the server, get rid of any typographical errors you might have made—I know I had a few—then run it:

```
npm run build  # or bsb -make-world
node src/Server.bs.js
```

You should get the message Listening at http://127.0.0.1:3000. Open up a browser, go to that URL, and you should see your test file displayed. (You can also use http://localhost:3000. It doesn't save any typing, but it involves fewer numbers.)

Now we need to create another similar route for any file name the user happens to enter. This route uses a route parameter (:filename). The actual file name the user enters is extracted from the request's param dictionary. The params() function returns a dictionary of Json.t, which is why the code needs to use Json.Decode.string():

interop/server/src/Server.re
```
Express.App.get(app, ~path="/:filename") @@
Express.Middleware.from((_, req) => {
  Express.Request.params(req)
  -> Js.Dict.unsafeGet("filename")
  -> Json.Decode.string
  -> Express.Response.sendFile(options(~root="./dist"))
});
```

There's something new here: the @@ operator. This is the *application operator*, and it's a way to call a function without using parentheses. For sqrt @@ 2 is the same as sqrt(2). Using @@ is helpful if you have deeply nested functions. These are equivalent:

```
let x = cos(sqrt(floor(5.7)));
let x = cos @@ sqrt @@ floor @@ 5.7;
```

In the server code, @@ avoids one extra set of parentheses and makes the code slightly more readable.

This is another good place for a test. Create another minimal HTML file with different content from index.html as dist/otherfile.html. Recompile and fire up the server again. Go to http://127.0.0.1:3000/otherfile.html in your browser. You should see that file's content.

Finally, the route we've all been waiting for... the route to handle XMLHttpRequests. We've given it the path /json, and we'll follow it with a query string that tells which column we want from the file of orders. For example, to retrieve the distribution of collar types, we'd go to the URL http://localhost:3000/json?choice=collar.

I'm putting this last in the explanation since it's conceptually the most complex, but this route *must* come before the /:filename route. Remember, Express tries routes in the order they occur, so we need to put the specific route /json before the /:filename route (which will match *any* single name).

interop/server/src/Server.re
```
Express.App.get(app, ~path="/json") @@
  Express.Middleware.from((_, req) => {
    Express.Request.query(req)
    -> Js.Dict.unsafeGet("choice")
    -> Json.Decode.string
    -> Stats.processFile("orders.csv", _)
    -> Express.Response.sendJson;
  });
```

This code uses the query() to get the client's choice of column and sends it to Stats.processFile(), which returns a JSON object that sendJson() returns to the client. The Stats code is a modified version of the solution that we asked you to create on page 125. You can see the full code at code/interop/server/src/Stats.re. The only part we'll show here is the section where we create a JSON object from a Belt.Map:

interop/server/src/Stats.re
```
let makeObject = (title: string, distribution: Belt.Map.t('k, 'v, 'id),
  toString: ('a) => string): Js.Json.t => {

  /* Create an array of pairs (key, value) from the distribution map */
  let pairs = Belt.Map.reduce(distribution, [| |],
    (acc, key, value) =>
      {Belt.Array.concat(acc, [|(toString(key), value)|])});

  /* Separate into two arrays */
  let (names, totals) = Belt.Array.unzip(pairs);

  /* And return a JSON object */
  E.object_([
    ("title", E.string(title)),
    ("choices", E.stringArray(names)),
    ("totals", E.array(E.int, totals))]);
};
```

There's one new thing in this code: Belt.Array.unzip(). This handy function takes an array of paired tuples and separates them into two arrays. For example:

```
let arr = [|("solid", 165), ("pinstripe", 153), ("check",82)|];
let (choices, totals) = Belt.Array.unzip(arr);
Js.log(choices); /* [|"solid", "pinstripe", "check"|] */
Js.log(totals); /* [|165, 153, 82|] */
```

You can test this code by entering this URL in your browser: http://local-host:3000/json?choice=color. You'll see the result come back in your browser's web console. If you haven't written the Stats.processFile() function yet but you still want to do some sort of test, send back an explicit JSON object:

```
let jsonObject = Json.Encode.object_([
  ("title", Json.Encode.string("Pattern")),
  ("choices", Json.Encode.stringArray([|"solid", "pinstripe", "check"|])),
  ("totals", Json.Encode.array(Json.Encode.int, [|165, 153, 82|]))]);
```

Implementing the Client

Now let's get the client side working. We'll need to use bs-webapi to access the DOM, bs-fetch to send data to the server and get a response, and bs-json to analyze the response. Create a project named client and install those libraries:

```
cd client
npm install --save bs-webapi
npm install --save bs-fetch
npm install --save @glennsl/bs-json
```

Remember to add the dependencies to the bsconfig.json file:

```
"bs-dependencies": [
  "bs-webapi",
  "bs-fetch",
  "@glennsl/bs-json"
],
```

Our HTML page will be just enough to get the job done: a <select> menu to select the summary we want, and a <div> to hold the resulting table:

```
interop/client/src/index.html
<!DOCTYPE html>
<html>
<head>
  <title>Shirt Statistics</title>
  <meta http-equiv="Content-Type" content="text/html; charset=utf-8" />
  <link rel="stylesheet" type="text/css" href="style.css"/>
</head>
<body>
  <h1>Shirt Statistics</h1>
  <p>
  <select id="category">
      <option value="">Select...</option>
```

```
        <option value="color">Color</option>
        <option value="size">Size</option>
        <option value="sleeve">Sleeve length</option>
        <option value="pattern">Pattern</option>
        <option value="cuff">Cuff</option>
        <option value="collar">Collar</option>
    </select>
  </p>

  <div id="resultTable"></div>

  <script type="text/javascript" src="Client.bs.js"></script>
  </body>
</html>
```

The ReasonML on the client side starts off with the definitions we used in Accessing the DOM, on page 49 and ends with the code that will send a request to the server when the selection menu changes:

interop/client/src/Client.re

```
module D = Webapi.Dom;
module Doc = Webapi.Dom.Document;
module Elem = Webapi.Dom.Element;

let getValue = (element: option(Elem.t)) : option(string) => {
  element
    -> Belt.Option.map(_, Elem.unsafeAsHtmlElement)
    -> Belt.Option.map(_, D.HtmlElement.value);
};

/* ... */

let category = Doc.getElementById("category", D.document);
switch (category) {
  | Some(element) =>
      D.EventTarget.addEventListener(
        "change", sendRequest, D.Element.asEventTarget(element))
  | None => ()
};
```

Here's the code for sending the request to the server:

interop/client/src/Client.re

```
Line 1  let sendRequest = (_: Dom.event) : unit => {
   -      let choice = getValue(Doc.getElementById("category", D.document));
   -      switch (choice) {
   -        | Some(choiceString) => {
   5            if (choiceString != "") {
   -              Fetch.fetchWithInit(
   -                "http://localhost:3000/json" ++ "?choice=" ++ choiceString,
   -                Fetch.RequestInit.make(~method_=Get, ()))
   -              )
   10             |> Js.Promise.then_(Fetch.Response.json)
```

```
        |> Js.Promise.then_(json => processResponse(json)
          |> Js.Promise.resolve)
        |> ignore;
      } else {
15        ()
      }
    }
  | None => ()
  };
20 };
```

We retrieve the select menu choice in line 2. If the choice isn't the empty
string, we use the fetchWithInit() to do an asynchronous GET request to a URL
with a query string that includes the selected choice (line 7). When the server
sends back the response, the first then_() call (line 10) will get the JSON
response, send it on to the processResponse(), and mark the promise as resolved.
This chain of calls uses pipe last (|>) because each of these calls wants the
value we're sending on as its last argument. We're not using the result for
any further calculation, so we pipe it to ignore() (line 13), which throws away
the result and returns unit.

Now it's time to handle the response from the server:

interop/client/src/Client.re
```
Line 1  module JD = Json.Decode;
      /* utility routines for creating HTML string */
      let capitalize = (s: string): string => {
        Js.String.toUpperCase(Js.String.get(s, 0)) ++
5        Js.String.toLowerCase(Js.String.substr(s, ~from=1))
      };

      let makeTableRow = (choice: string, total:int): string => {
        "<tr><td>" ++ choice ++ "</td><td>"
10      ++ string_of_int(total) ++ "</td></tr>\n"
      };

      let processResponse = (json: Js.Json.t): unit =>
      {
15      let optResult = Doc.getElementById("resultTable", D.document);

        switch (optResult) {
        | Some(resultElement) => {
            let title = JD.field("title", JD.string, json);
20          let choices = JD.field("choices", JD.array(JD.string), json);
            let totals = JD.field("totals", JD.array(JD.int), json);
            let htmlStr = "<table><thead><tr><th>" ++ capitalize(title)
              ++ "</th><th>Total</th></tr>\n"
              ++ Belt.Array.reduce(Belt.Array.zip(choices, totals), "",
25            (acc, (choice, total)) => acc ++ makeTableRow(choice, total))
              ++ "</table>\n";
```

```
        Elem.setInnerHTML(resultElement, htmlStr);
      }
    | None => ()
30  }
};
```

The server's response—the JSON data—is ready for us in the parameter. If we found the element where our HTML table will go (line 18), we convert the JSON object to ReasonML data starting in line 19 and create an HTML string with the table of results (line 22). That code uses Belt.Array.zip(), which is the opposite of the unzip() function: it takes two arrays and combines them into a single array of paired tuples.   (If we didn't find the element for the HTML table, the None case in line 29 returns unit and does nothing.)

Line 27 deposits our HTML into the result table <div>.

We now build the client code, bundle it up with parcel, and—here's the key—move the resulting dist folder to the server project's directory so we can test the whole client/server system. Presume we're in the client directory with the following directory structure. (The server/dist directory was created when we tested the server. You *did* test the server first, didn't you?)

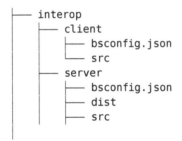

```
├── interop
│   ├── client
│   │   ├── bsconfig.json
│   │   └── src
│   ├── server
│   │   ├── bsconfig.json
│   │   ├── dist
│   │   ├── src
│   │
```

Here's the sequence of commands that I described. I found myself doing this sequence of commands so often that I created a bash shell script to save some typing. You might wish to do likewise.

```
npm run build
# Create bundle in client/dist directory
parcel build src/index.html --public-url ./ --no-minify
# Remove old server/dist directory
rm -rf ../server/dist
# Transfer newly-built client code to server area
mv dist ../server
```

Now restart the server (if it's not already running), go to http://localhost:3000/, and enjoy your spiffy new table-maker.

It's Your Turn

Okay, tables aren't *that* spiffy. Charts are a lot more attractive, so your task in this exercise is to create a new client project that uses Chart.js.[8] Again, I'm explaining just enough of that library to help you write the bindings you need to create a horizontal bar chart for the shirt statistics. If you feel energized and want to write a complete set of bindings for Chart.js, make sure you share it with the rest of us when you finish.

You'll need to install Chart.js with npm install --save chart.js. This will add an entry to the dependencies in your package.json file. You don't have to add it to the dependencies in bsconfig.json.

Here's a summary of the information you need to draw a horizontal bar chart. You create a chart by calling the Chart object constructor with two parameters. The first parameter is a DOM element reference to a <canvas> element. The second parameter is a rather deeply nested object describing the graph data and appearance, which we'll go over in a bit. The constructor creates the chart and displays it on the canvas.

Before you can draw another chart on the canvas, you have to free all the data structures that Chart.js is using for the current chart. You do that by calling the destroy() method of the Chart object you constructed. This means you have to do something we haven't done before: create a global variable that can change.

Working with Mutable Variables

The norm in ReasonML is to presume that variables are immutable. Functions in Belt.Array treat ReasonML arrays as immutable—the functions return a new array, leaving the argument untouched, even though the underlying JavaScript arrays are mutable. To create a mutable variable, you need to wrap it in a ref. Here's code that creates a global variable for a person's age, and accesses and changes it:

```
let age: ref(int) = ref(22);

let birthday = (a: ref(int)): unit => {
  a := a^ + 1
}

birthday(age);
Js.log(age^); /* 23 */
```

---

8. www.chartjs.org/

To access the content of a ref variable, follow its name with an circumflex (^). To assign a value to a ref variable, use :=, which updates the content of the reference, rather than =, which creates a binding between a name and value.

Here's the code I used to create a global variable for the chart and update it:

interop/graphic-client/src/GraphicClient.re
```
let theChart: ref(option(Chart.t)) = ref(None);
/* ... */
```

Let's get back to the second parameter of the Chart constructor—the deeply nested object that describes the chart. In short, it specifies:

- The labels for the bars
- One or more data sets, which consist of:
    - The label for the data set
    - The data values
    - The background color, border color, and border width for the bars
- Options that specify whether the graph is responsive or not, and how to scale the *x* and *y* axes

Here's an example of what that object looks like:

```
{
  type: "horizontalBar",
  data: {
    labels: ["Red", "Green", "Blue"], // labels for the bars
    datasets: [ // an array of objects, each describing a set of data
      {
        label: "label for set of data",
        data: [20, 30, 40], // data points
        backgroundColor: [ // fill color for bars
          "rgba(255, 0, 0, 0.5)",
          "rgba(0, 255, 0, 0.5)",
          "rgba(0, 0, 255, 0.5)"
        ],
        borderColor: [ // border color for bars
          "#ff0000",
          "#008000",
          "#0000ff",
        ],
        borderWidth: 1 // integer
      }
    ]
  },
  options: {
    legend: {
      display: false, // display data set label
    },
    responsive: false,
```

```
    scales: {
      xAxes: [{ // array of objects
        ticks: {
          beginAtZero:true
        }
      }],
      yAxes: []
    }
  }
}
```

A few notes: if you specify fewer background colors than there are bars, the remaining bars will be 50% transparent gray. If you specify fewer border colors than bars, the bars will have no border. Colors can be specified in any CSS-compatible format. In the options object, you must set responsive to false for the graph to be sized to the area of your <canvas>. It's possible to have multiple axes (useful if there are multiple data sets), which is why xAxes and yAxes are arrays. If you specify an empty array for an axis, as we did for yAxes, Chart.js doesn't do anything special for that axis.

There are a lot of objects here, so you're going to be creating a lot of types with [@bs.deriving abstract]. I strongly suggest you put all your Chart.js types and bindings in a separate file named Chart.re. I also recommend that you put each type in its own module to avoid name collisions. It's possible to nest modules. But again, for readability, I wouldn't recommend nesting too deeply:

interop/graphic-client/src/Chart.re
```
module Axis = {
  module Tickmark = {
    [@bs.deriving abstract] type t = {
      beginAtZero: bool
    };
  };
  [@bs.deriving abstract] type t = {
    ticks: Tickmark.t
  };
};
```

You can see the full code in directory code/interop/graphic-client/src.

Summing Up

You now have the basics of interoperating with JavaScript: binding to Java-Script functions, working with JavaScript objects, and encoding and decoding JSON. For the full details of BuckleScript/ReasonML's extensive interop capabilities, see bucklescript.github.io/docs/en/interop-overview.

You may have noticed in Working with Mutable Variables, on page 137 my reluctance—bordering on distaste—for talking about mutable objects and, in particular, mutable global state. This is an issue that bothers many people who are used to the functional programming style, and some exceptionally bright programmers have come up with an answer: reactive programming. That's what we'll investigate in the next chapter.

CHAPTER 9

Making Applications with Reason/React

Learning React will make it far easier for you to develop web applications. First, React will take care of the DOM manipulation. You can say goodbye to all the work we had to do to make sure that we were dealing with a Dom.HtmlElement instead of Dom.Element.t. Second, your code will be better organized. React lets you tie together a DOM element and the code that manipulates it as a *component*. It's easier to modify your application when your web page is composed of these building blocks instead of a monolithic mass of code and data. React lets you create more complex, powerful web applications with the same or less effort than you would need if using plain ReasonML with the DOM.

Viewing React from 20,000 Meters

This section is written for those of us who haven't used React or aren't familiar with it. (Yes, that includes me.)

React lets you think of a web page as consisting of components. A component accepts input (*properties*, also called *props*) and returns "React elements describing what should appear on the screen."[1] You can write these as functions, or you can use a notation called JSX, an extension to JavaScript that lets you write HTML-like expressions mixed in with JavaScript code. ReasonML also lets you use JSX-style notation that contains ReasonML code.

An example of a component might be a Notice component with properties that describe the message text, the color of the text, and the icon to display with the message. In JSX, that might look like:

```
<Notice message="Variable y is not defined"
  color="#880000" icon="notice_icons/error.svg" />
```

---

1. reactjs.org/docs/components-and-props.html

To address the problem of global state, you can have what React calls *stateful components*. A stateful component contains a JavaScript object whose fields describe the component's current status. We could, for example, revise the preceding chapter's graphic example on page 138 to use a FrequencyChart component, where the Chart.t object is part of the component rather than a global variable.

Components can have event-handling code that updates their state, and components can contain other components.

Once you have your components, you tell React to *render* them into a web page. React keeps track of everything, displaying the components and updating them as events occur, as specified by your code. The most magical part of React is that it updates *only* the parts of the page that need updating, rather than updating the entire page's DOM. That's the idea of React in a nutshell, and its power is now available to you in ReasonML. You may find Dan Abramov's explanation of React components, elements, and instances to be informative as well.[2]

Other Frameworks

 React isn't the only game in town. There are other frameworks that provide similar capabilities, which also use a *reactive programming* approach. Among the options are Vue,[3] Angular,[4] and Preact.[5]

Starting a ReasonReact Project

As specified in the ReasonReact web site[6], you start a project with ReasonReact like this:

```
bsb -init react-test -theme react
cd react-test
```

Here's the directory structure it creates:

```
├── bsconfig.json
├── node_modules
│   └── bs-platform
├── package.json
├── README.md
```

---

2. reactjs.org/blog/2015/12/18/react-components-elements-and-instances.html
3. vuejs.org/
4. angular.io/
5. preactjs.com/
6. reasonml.github.io/reason-react/docs/en/installation

```
├── src
│   ├── Component1.re
│   ├── Component2.re
│   ├── index.html
│   └── Index.re
└── webpack.config.js
```

The main differences between this project and non-React projects are that the src directory contains some sample components and an HTML file. We'll look at the source files more closely later. There's also webpack.config.js which, as its name suggests, is a configuration file for the webpack[7] bundler. This is the default bundler for ReasonReact projects, so we'll be using it instead of parcel, as we did on page 49.

Now let's install the dependencies that a React project needs. This step will take a while, and it will install *many* things in the node_modules directory, but you'll only need to do it once:

```
npm install
```

Then compile the project with an option to monitor files and recompile whenever a source file changes:

```
npm start
```

Go to another terminal window and issue the following command, which runs webpack to create a bundle we can run and it also watches for file changes:

```
npm run webpack
```

If you open yet another terminal window and look at the file structure, you'll see a new directory:

```
├── build
│   ├── index.html
│   └── Index.js
```

You can go to your browser and open the index.html file (no server required). You'll see this rather plain-looking page:

---

7. webpack.js.org/

As we'll see when we look at the code, the first component is stateless—it conveys a static message. If you open your web console and click on the word "Hello!", you should see the word "clicked" appear in the console. The second component is stateful—it keeps track of the number of clicks on the left button and whether the greeting following the right button should be visible or not.

Investigating the Sample Project

The index.html file has two <div> elements with id= attributes. The Index.re file renders (displays) the components in those <div>s.

reason-react/react-test/src/index.html

```
<!DOCTYPE html>
<html lang="en">
<head>
  <meta charset="UTF-8">
  <title>ReasonReact Examples</title>
</head>
<body>
  Component 1:
  <div id="index1"></div>

  Component 2:
  <div id="index2"></div>

  <script src="Index.js"></script>
</body>
</html>
```

reason-react/react-test/src/Index.re

```
ReactDOMRe.renderToElementWithId(<Component1 message="Hello!" />, "index1");

ReactDOMRe.renderToElementWithId(<Component2 greeting="Hello!" />, "index2");
```

What's this code <Component1 message="Hello!" /> that looks like an HTML tag? That's JSX, and it's shorthand for this code:

```
ReasonReact.element(Component1.make(~message="Hello!",[|||]))
```

The properties of the component—in this case, the only property—become labeled parameters to make(). The last argument is an array of child components, which is unused in this case. Let's take a look at the Component1 module and flesh out the comments in the file.

reason-react/react-test/src/Component1.re

```
Line 1  /* This is the basic component. */
    -   let component = ReasonReact.statelessComponent("Component1");

    -   /* Your familiar handleClick from ReactJS. This mandatorily takes the payload,
    5       then the `self` record, which contains state (none here), `handle`, `reduce`
    -       and other utilities */
```

```
     let handleClick = (_event, _self) => Js.log("clicked!");

     /* `make` is the function that mandatorily takes `children` (if you want to use
10      `JSX). `message` is a named argument, which simulates ReactJS props. Usage:

        `<Component1 message="hello" />`

        Which desugars to
15
        `ReasonReact.element(Component1.make(~message="hello", [|||]))` */
     let make = (~message, _children) => {
       ...component,
       render: self =>
20       <div onClick=(self.handle(handleClick))>
           {ReasonReact.string(message)}
         </div>,
     };
```

The argument to ReasonReact.statelessComponent() in line 2 is a string that's used for debugging, console logging, and error messages. It can have any value you want. A very good choice is _MODULE_, which the compiler replaces with the name of the module.[8]

This component doesn't do anything in response to clicks except log the fact that you clicked the greeting, so line 7 doesn't need to use either of its arguments. The leading underscore prevents "unused variable" messages.

The component really gets down to business in line 17. make() is a function that takes as its argument the component's property (or properties) and an array of child components. In this case, the single property is ~message (the value of the JSX message= attribute). We don't need to access the children—there aren't any—so again, we use a leading underscore.

This function returns an ordinary ReasonML record with all the current fields of the component (using the ... spread operator) and a new value for the render field. The value for render is a function that takes a single argument, self, which is essentially the equivalent of JavaScript's this, and returns the React elements to be rendered. Expressions in braces are evaluated when the component is rendered.

First, let's look at line 21, which displays the message. We can't use {message} because items being rendered must be React elements. ReasonReact.string() converts the ReasonML string to a React element. There is also a ReasonReact.array() function that converts a ReasonML array to a React element.

---

8.   reasonml.github.io/api/Pervasives.html#VAL__MODULE__

Newer Versions of the Template

In older versions of the template, the comments starting in line 8 refer to Page. This is a mistype. The component name is Component1. ReasonML also allows you to have single expressions in parentheses rather than braces, with braces reserved for blocks of code. This book shows an updated version of the template that has the mistype corrected and uses braces throughout. But as of this writing, it may not yet be in your installation of ReasonML.

Event names in JSX use camel case. Line 20 uses onClick rather than the all lowercase onclick you would see in JavaScript.

Creating a More Complex Stateless Component

After reading this, you might be thinking, "Okay, I got this." I thought that, too. Then I decided to create the Notice component I mentioned earlier in the chapter. I soon realized that no, I don't "got this," because there are a *lot* of new things we need to make this component happen. Let's dive in!

First, the figure on page 147 shows what we want the notices to look like when they grow up. The notice box will need styling to get the border and the vertically aligned text.

We'll put the icons, which are in SVG format, into a directory named notice_icons at the top level of our project directory:

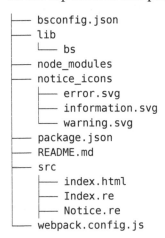

```
├── bsconfig.json
├── lib
│   └── bs
├── node_modules
├── notice_icons
│   ├── error.svg
│   ├── information.svg
│   └── warning.svg
├── package.json
├── README.md
├── src
│   ├── index.html
│   ├── Index.re
│   ├── Notice.re
└── webpack.config.js
```

When we bundle with webpack, it processes JavaScript files (compiled from ReasonML) and HTML files, but it doesn't know how to deal with image files.

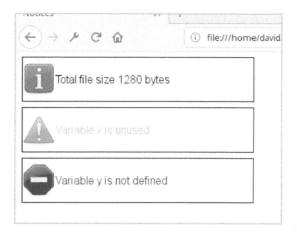

We have to install the file-loader module,[9] using the --save-dev option. This indicates that file-loader is a developer-time dependency, not to be included in production.

```
npm install file-loader --save-dev
```

Next, we must inform webpack when to use file-loader by adding this to our webpack.config.js file:

reason-react/notices/webpack.config.js
```
Line 1  plugins: [
          new HtmlWebpackPlugin({
            template: 'src/index.html',
            inject: false
     5    })
        ],
        module: {
          rules: [
            {
    10        test: /\.(png|jpg|svg)$/,
              use: [
                {
                  loader: 'file-loader',
                  options: {
    15              name: '[path][name].[ext]'
                  }
                }
              ]
            }
    20    ]
        },
        devServer: {
```

---

9. github.com/webpack-contrib/file-loader

The code we've added starts in line 7. We use a regular expression in line 10 to specify that files ending in .png, .jpg, and .svg should use the file loader (line 13). The loader will copy the files to the bundle with the path name (relative to the top of our project), the file name, and its extension (line 15). This means that the icons will be in a directory named notice_icons, that lives in the same directory as the bundled HTML and JavaScript files:

```
build
├── index.html
├── Index.js
└── notice_icons
    ├── error.svg
    ├── information.svg
    └── warning.svg
```

Now that the housekeeping is out of the way, let's turn our attention to the code. The index.html file is pretty much the same as the sample, with three <div> elements to hold our Notice components:

reason-react/notices/src/index.html

```html
<!DOCTYPE html>
<html lang="en">
<head>
  <meta charset="UTF-8">
  <title>Notices</title>
</head>
<body>

  <div id="info"></div>
  <div id="warn"></div>
  <div id="err"></div>

  <script src="Index.js"></script>
</body>
</html>
```

Similarly, there's not a lot new in our Index.re file, which renders one of each type of Notice to the appropriate <div>:

reason-react/notices/src/Index.re

```
ReactDOMRe.renderToElementWithId(
  <Notice message="Total file size 1280 bytes"
    color="#000" icon="information" />, "info");

ReactDOMRe.renderToElementWithId(
  <Notice message="Variable x is unused"
    color="#FF8C00" icon="warning" />, "warn");

ReactDOMRe.renderToElementWithId(
  <Notice message="Variable y is not defined"
    color="#8B0000" icon="error" />, "err");
```

However, when we get to the component itself in Notice.re, you'll see a lot of new things.

```
reason-react/notices/src/Notice.re
[@bs.val] external require : string => string = "";

require("../notice_icons/warning.svg");
require("../notice_icons/error.svg");
require("../notice_icons/information.svg");

let component = ReasonReact.statelessComponent("Notice");

let noticeStyle = (color) =>
  ReactDOMRe.Style.make(
    ~color=color, ~clear="left",
    ~minHeight="64px", ~marginBottom="0.5em",
    ~width="30%", ~display="flex", ~alignItems="center",
    ~border="1px solid black", ());

let make =  (~message, ~color, ~icon, _children) => {
  ...component,
  render: _self =>
    <div style={noticeStyle(color)}>
      <img src={"notice_icons/" ++ icon ++ ".svg"}
        style = {ReactDOMRe.Style.make(~width="48px", ~float="left", ())} />
      {ReasonReact.string(message)}
    </div>,
};
```

First, we have to require() the SVG files. This lets webpack know that it has to process them. We give the paths relative to the source file, which is why the paths start with ../.

To make the code more readable, we put the creation of the styling information for the component in a separate function starting on line 10. The ReactDOM-Re.Style.make() function uses labeled parameters for the style properties. CSS hyphenated names such as min-height, margin-bottom, and align-items become the camel case minHeight, marginBottom, and alignItems.

In line 16, the make() function has three properties plus the (unused) _children parameter. The style function is called in line 19 to provide a value for the style= attribute.

The SVG file is included as an <img>, and we build the file name in line 20 by concatenating the directory name—where the images will be after the bundle is built, the icon string, and the .svg extension.

Lastly, line 22 provides the message, expressed as a ReasonReact.string().

It's Your Turn

Create an <Animal species="..." name="..."> component that renders as a PNG of an animal of the given species, with the specified name below the image. The starting point for this project is in the code/reason-react/animal-component directory. Here is the index.html file and the style.css that it refers to:

reason-react/animal-component/src/index.html

```html
<!DOCTYPE html>
<html lang="en">
<head>
  <meta charset="UTF-8">
  <title>ReasonReact and file-loader</title>
  <link rel="stylesheet" type="text/css" href="style.css"/>
</head>
<body>
  <div class="horiz" id="image1"></div>
  <div class="horiz" id="image2"></div>
  <div class="horiz" id="image3"></div>
  <div class="horiz" id="image4"></div>

  <script src="Index.js"></script>
</body>
</html>
```

reason-react/animal-component/src/style.css

```css
div.horiz {
  display: inline-block;
}
```

The images are in directory code/reason-react/animal-component/images. When the program is finished, the web page should look like this:

The starting point for the <Animal> component is in code/reason-react/animal-component/src/Animal.re. You will also need to make changes to code/reason-react/animal-component/webpack.config.js.

One solution is in directory code/reason-react/animal-component-complete.

Using Stateful Components

The Component1, Notice, and Animal components all have one thing in common—the properties completely define everything we need to render the component. On the other hand, Component2 in the template, which defines a *stateful* component, has to keep track of the number of times the left button has been clicked and whether the text is visible or not. The component starts out with a definition of a type that reflects this information:

reason-react/react-test/src/Component2.re
```
/* State declaration */
type state = {
  count: int,
  show: bool,
};
```

The state of the component is changed in response to user actions, which we define in the action type:

reason-react/react-test/src/Component2.re
```
/* Action declaration */
type action =
  | Click
  | Toggle;
```

We can then create a reducerComponent (rather than a statelessComponent) and its make() function:

reason-react/react-test/src/Component2.re
```
Line 1  /* Component template declaration.
           Needs to be **after** state and action declarations! */
      - let component =
      -     ReasonReact.reducerComponent("Example");
      5
      - /* greeting and children are props. `children` isn't used, therefore ignored.
      -    We ignore it by prepending it with an underscore */
      - let make =
      -     (~greeting, _children) => {
     10  /* spread the other default fields of component here and override a few */
      - ...component,
      -
      - initialState: () => {count: 0, show: true},
      -
     15  /* State transitions */
      - reducer: (action, state) =>
      -   switch (action) {
      -   | Click => ReasonReact.Update({...state, count: state.count + 1})
      -   | Toggle => ReasonReact.Update({...state, show: ! state.show})
     20   },
      -
```

```
     render: self => {
       let message =
         "You've clicked this " ++ string_of_int(self.state.count) ++ " times(s)";
25     <div>
         <button onClick={_event => self.send(Click)}>
           {ReasonReact.string(message)}
         </button>
         <button onClick={_event => self.send(Toggle)}>
30         {ReasonReact.string("Toggle greeting")}
         </button>
         {self.state.show ? ReasonReact.string(greeting) : ReasonReact.null}
       </div>;
     },
35 };
```

In addition to the render field, we have to create the initial state of the component in line 13. Notice that init() is a function with no arguments that returns a record. The reducer field in line 16 uses ReasonReact.Update() to return a new state in response to actions. The actions are initiated by the send() function when events occur (lines 26 and 29).

Putting Components Together

Let's use our shirt data structure to create a web page that lets you specify shirt orders and put them in a table. Here's what it looks like after adding three valid orders and trying to add an order with a negative quantity:

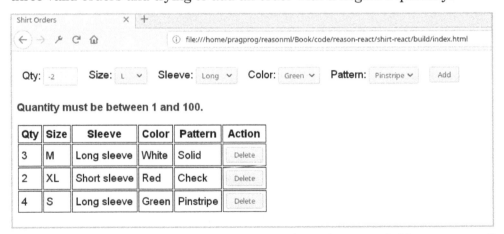

The data entry form, which holds the strings from the input fields, an array of the orders entered so far, and the error message to display, will be the responsibility of a single stateful OrderForm component whose state looks like this:

```
reason-react/shirt-react/src/OrderForm.re
type state = {
  qtyStr: string,
  sizeStr: string,
  sleeveStr: string,
  colorStr: string,
  patternStr: string,
  nextOrderNumber: int,
  orders: array(Shirt.Order.t),
  errorText: string,
};
```

There's an extra field in this record, nextOrderNumber, used to keep track of which orderNumber to assign to the orders the user enters.

The order record is very much like the one we've seen in Chapter 7, Structuring Data with Records and Modules, on page 103, and it is represented by a stateless OrderItem component that renders an order as a table row:

```
reason-react/shirt-react/src/Shirt.re
module Order = {
  type t = {
    orderNumber: int,
    quantity: int,
    size: Size.t,
    sleeve: Sleeve.t,
    color: Color.t,
    pattern: Pattern.t,
  }
};
```

To save space, we've omitted the Cuff and Collar types, and we've added an orderNumber field to distinguish among otherwise identical records. We've also changed the toString() functions—not shown here to save space—to return capitalized strings.

Conceptually, the OrderForm will contain OrderItem components:

```
<OrderForm>
  <OrderItem ...>
  <OrderItem ...>
</OrderForm>
```

The OrderItem Component

Here's the code for the OrderItem component:

```
                 reason-react/shirt-react/src/OrderItem.re
Line 1   module RR = ReasonReact;

         let component = RR.statelessComponent("OrderItem");

   5     let make = (~order: Shirt.Order.t,
                     ~deleteFunction: (ReactEvent.Mouse.t) => unit, _children) =>
         {
           ...component,

  10        render: (_self) => {
             <tr>
               <td>{RR.string(string_of_int(order.quantity))}</td>
               <td>{RR.string(Shirt.Size.toString(order.size))}</td>
               <td>{RR.string(Shirt.Sleeve.toString(order.sleeve))}</td>
  15           <td>{RR.string(Shirt.Color.toString(order.color))}</td>
               <td>{RR.string(Shirt.Pattern.toString(order.pattern))}</td>
               <td>
                 <button onClick={deleteFunction}>{RR.string("Delete")}</button>
               </td>
  20
             </tr>
           }
         };
```

Line 1 saves us some typing.

The render() function starting in line 10 creates a series of table cells from the order fields. Things get interesting when we create the button in line 18. What is this deleteFunction, and why is it one of our parameters in line 7? Why didn't we just define a function in this component that modifies the parent OrderForm component? The answer is: we can't. React has *unidirectional data flow*. Child components get a read-only version of the parent's state. If the child needs to communicate with the parent, it has to do so via a function provided by the parent. In this case, that's the deleteFunction property of the OrderItem. We'll see how it's implemented when we look at the OrderForm component.

The OrderForm Component

There is only one new ReasonML feature in this code, so most of the explanation will be about React features. We start off with functions to convert from strings to data types, with default values in case the conversions fail:

```
               reason-react/shirt-react/src/OrderForm.re
let convertWithDefault = (str: string, defaultValue: 'a,
                          convert: (string) => option('a)): 'a => {
  Belt.Option.getWithDefault(convert(str), defaultValue);
};
```

```
let toIntWithDefault = (s:string, defaultValue:int): int => {
  switch (int_of_string(s)) {
    | result => result
    | exception(Failure("int_of_string")) => defaultValue
  }
};
```

Here are the state (which we saw earlier in this chapter) and the actions: we can either enter an order, change the fields of an order, or delete an existing order:

reason-react/shirt-react/src/OrderForm.re
```
type state = {
  qtyStr: string,
  sizeStr: string,
  sleeveStr: string,
  colorStr: string,
  patternStr: string,
  nextOrderNumber: int,
  orders: array(Shirt.Order.t),
  errorText: string,
};
```

reason-react/shirt-react/src/OrderForm.re
```
type action =
  | Enter(Shirt.Order.t)
  | ChangeQty(string)
  | ChangeSize(string)
  | ChangeSleeve(string)
  | ChangeColor(string)
  | ChangePattern(string)
  | Delete(Shirt.Order.t);
```

The Change... variants have a string parameter that will come from the value of the text field and the drop-down menus.

We have to create several <select> menus, so let's write a function that takes the menu label, an array of menu choices, the currently selected value, and a function that's invoked whenever the menu's value changes:

reason-react/shirt-react/src/OrderForm.re
```
Line 1  let makeSelect = (label: string, choices: array(string),
                         value: string, changeFcn) => {

        let makeOptionElement = (value: string) => {
   5      <option key={value} value={value}>{ReasonReact.string(value)}</option>
        };

        let menuOptionElements = Belt.Array.map(choices, makeOptionElement);
  10
```

```
    <span className="item">
      <label>{ReasonReact.string(" " ++ label ++ ": ")}</label>
      <select value={value} onChange={changeFcn}>
        {ReasonReact.array(menuOptionElements)}
15    </select>
    </span>
};
```

The makeOptionElement() function creates an individual <element> from a value. The key= attribute in line 5 is a special attribute for React to help it "identify which items have changed, are added, or are removed".[10]

The call to Belt.Array.map() in line 8 produces an array of <option> elements. We can't put an ordinary array into the <select> element—we have to convert it to a ReasonReact.array in line 14.

To set the CSS class of the <span> element in line 11, we use className= instead of the reserved word class.

When the user clicks the Add button, we will gather the data from the state and create a Shirt.order.t record with the next available order number:

reason-react/shirt-react/src/OrderForm.re
```
let createOrder = (state) : Shirt.Order.t => {
  {
    orderNumber: state.nextOrderNumber,
    quantity: toIntWithDefault(state.qtyStr, 0),
    size: convertWithDefault(state.sizeStr, Shirt.Size.Medium,
                             Shirt.Size.fromString),
    sleeve: convertWithDefault(state.sleeveStr, Shirt.Sleeve.Long,
                               Shirt.Sleeve.fromString),
    color: convertWithDefault(state.colorStr, Shirt.Color.White,
                              Shirt.Color.fromString),
    pattern: convertWithDefault(state.patternStr, Shirt.Pattern.Solid,
                                Shirt.Pattern.fromString),
  }
};
```

Let's move on to the make() function, which starts off by defining an initialState. The strings will get overwritten as the user changes fields, so I chose what seemed to be reasonable defaults. There are no orders yet, the nextOrderNumber will be 1, and there's no errorText to display:

reason-react/shirt-react/src/OrderForm.re
```
let component = ReasonReact.reducerComponent("OrderForm");

let make = (_children) => {
  ...component,
```

---

10. reactjs.org/docs/lists-and-keys.html#keys

```
initialState: () => {
  qtyStr: "1",
  sizeStr: Shirt.Size.toString(Shirt.Size.Medium),
  sleeveStr: Shirt.Sleeve.toString(Shirt.Sleeve.Long),
  colorStr: Shirt.Color.toString(Shirt.Color.White),
  patternStr: Shirt.Pattern.toString(Shirt.Pattern.Solid),
  orders: [| |],
  nextOrderNumber: 1,
  errorText: ""
},
```

Next, let's examine the reducer function's code for the Enter action.

reason-react/shirt-react/src/OrderForm.re

```
Line 1  reducer: (action, state:state) =>
   -      switch (action) {
   -      | Enter(order) => {
   -          let n = toIntWithDefault(state.qtyStr, 0);
   5          if (n > 0 && n <= 100) {
   -            ReasonReact.Update({...state,
   -              orders: Belt.Array.concat(state.orders, [|order|]),
   -              nextOrderNumber: state.nextOrderNumber + 1,
   -              errorText: ""
  10            })
   -          } else {
   -            ReasonReact.Update({...state,
   -              errorText: "Quantity must be between 1 and 100."
   -            })
  15          }
   -        }
```

If the quantity ordered is in a valid range, we update the state (line 6) by concatenating the order to the orders array (line 7), updating the nextOrderNumber (line 8) and clearing the errorText (line 9), which might have been set by invalid data (line 13) in a previous entry.

The Change... actions all follow the same pattern: update the corresponding string in the state. Here is the code for changing the quantity and shirt size. The remaining actions follow this same pattern:

reason-react/shirt-react/src/OrderForm.re

```
| ChangeQty(newQty) => {
    ReasonReact.Update({...state, qtyStr: newQty})
  }
| ChangeSize(newSize) => {
    ReasonReact.Update({...state, sizeStr: newSize})
  }
```

The Delete action updates the state by keeping all the orders except the one whose order number matches the one we want to delete:

reason-react/shirt-react/src/OrderForm.re

```
| Delete(order) => {
    ReasonReact.Update({...state,
    orders: Belt.Array.keep(state.orders,
            (item) => (item.orderNumber != order.orderNumber))})
  }
```

The render function is rather lengthy because it has to display a lot of things, so let's analyze it in parts. We create a variable orderItems of all the <OrderItem> components.

reason-react/shirt-react/src/OrderForm.re

```
render: self => {
  let orderItems = Belt.Array.map(self.state.orders, (order) =>
      <OrderItem key={string_of_int(order.orderNumber)}
        order={order} deleteFunction=(_event => self.send(Delete(order)))/>);
```

There are two things to notice here. First, the key= attribute. React insists on each array element having a unique key= property, and the order numbers are unique. Second, the assignment of the deleteFunction property. It's an anonymous function that sends the form a Delete action. This is the answer to the question we asked on page 154 about how the child can communicate with the parent. We're defining this anonymous function in OrderForm. The function will become the onClick= handler of the child OrderItem's button. When the OrderItem's button is clicked, the call it makes is to a function belonging to the parent, which has access to OrderForm's state.

Next, we create an orderTable variable that renders the table if there are orders. Again, it has to convert the orderItems array to a ReasonReact.array:

reason-react/shirt-react/src/OrderForm.re

```
let orderTable =
  if (Belt.Array.length(self.state.orders) > 0) {
    <table>
     <thead>
       <tr>
         <th>{ReasonReact.string("Qty")}</th>
         <th>{ReasonReact.string("Size")}</th>
         <th>{ReasonReact.string("Sleeve")}</th>
         <th>{ReasonReact.string("Color")}</th>
         <th>{ReasonReact.string("Pattern")}</th>
         <th>{ReasonReact.string("Action")}</th>
       </tr>
     </thead>
     <tbody>
       {ReasonReact.array(orderItems)}
     </tbody>
    </table>
  } else {
```

```
    <p>
      {ReasonReact.string("No orders entered yet.")}
    </p>
};
```

Now we turn our attention to the form fields, starting with the input field for the quantity:

reason-react/shirt-react/src/OrderForm.re

```
Line 1  <div>
     2    <p className="flex">
     3    <span className="item">
     4      {ReasonReact.string("Qty: ")}
     5      <input type_="text" size=4
     6        value={self.state.qtyStr}
     7        onChange={(event)=>
     8          self.send(ChangeQty(ReactEvent.Form.target(event)##value))}/>
     9    </span>
```

The content of the field is set in line 6. We create an onChange handler as an anonymous function in line 7. This function takes the triggering event as its parameter and sends a ChangeQty action. The argument to ChangeQty (line 8) is the value of the target event. This line contains a new operator: ##, which is used to access a field in a JavaScript object. (We can't use a function like valueGet() as we did on page 124 because ReasonReact hasn't done a [@bs.deriving abstract] for the target event.)

The select menus all follow the same pattern. They set the menu value from the appropriate string in the state, and they have an anonymous function that invokes the corresponding Change...() function when the user selects a different item. To save space, I am showing only one of these functions:

reason-react/shirt-react/src/OrderForm.re

```
Line 1  {makeSelect("Size",
     2    [|"XS", "S", "M", "L", "XL", "XXL", "XXXL"|],
     3    self.state.sizeStr,
     4    (event) => self.send(ChangeSize(
     5      ReactEvent.Form.target(event)##value)))}
```

Finally, we define the <button>, the error text field, and the table of orders:

reason-react/shirt-react/src/OrderForm.re

```
Line 1    <span className="item">
     -      <button onClick=(_event => {
     -        let order = createOrder(self.state);
     -        self.send(Enter(order))}) >
     5        {ReasonReact.string("Add")}
     -      </button>
     -    </span>
     -    </p>
```

```
10    <p id="errorText">
        {ReasonReact.string(self.state.errorText)}
      </p>

      {orderTable}
15  </div>;
```

It's Your Turn

Let's modify this program. First, change the select menus so that they contain the menu label, as shown here:

Unlike the current program, which keeps the state of the form after you click the Add button, the modified program will reset the menus to show the labels and clear out the quantity field after adding a record.

In the current program, once you add an order to the list, you can't edit it—you have to delete it and create a new order. Your task is to modify the current program so that you can edit any entry in the table. While you're editing an order, the selected row should be highlighted, and the Add button should change to read "Update." When you click that button, the table row needs to un-highlight and the button once again should be Add. An order in the process of being edited might look like this:

Here are some things I had to do while implementing these modifications:

- Add styles for a normal and edited table row to index.html.

- Remove <label> elements from index.html.

- Add editFunction= (callback to parent) and editing= (boolean) properties to the OrderItem component.

- Add an option(int) in the state that tells which order number is being edited.

- Add an action for missing data (quantity not entered or drop-downs not chosen).

- Because data can be missing, have the createOrder() function return an option(Shirt.Order.t).

- Copy the map2() function on page 113 to help deal with option values.

- Because the Enter(order) action checks if the order is being added or edited —if edited, have the code replace the order rather than append it to state.orders.

Adding Side Effects with Storage

Let's use this new, improved shirt order program as the base for our final example in this chapter. We'll store the state of the page in the browser's local storage[11] in JSON format.

We'll need to include @glennsl/bs-json in our bsconfig.json and install it via npm install --save @glennsl/bs-json, as we did on page 126:

```
"bs-dependencies": [
    "reason-react",
    "@glennsl/bs-json"
],
```

We need to add code to convert to and from JSON. First, let's look at the Order type in file Shirt.re. The new entries here are the encodeJson() and decodeJson() functions:

reason-react/shirt-storage/src/Shirt.re
```
module E = Json.Encode;
module D = Json.Decode;

module Order = {
  type t = {
    orderNumber: int,
```

---

11. developer.mozilla.org/en-US/docs/Web/API/Storage/LocalStorage

```
    quantity: int,
    size: Size.t,
    sleeve: Sleeve.t,
    color: Color.t,
    pattern: Pattern.t,
  };
  let encodeJson = (order: t): Js.Json.t => {
   E.object_([
   ("orderNumber", E.int(order.orderNumber)),
   ("quantity", E.int(order.quantity)),
   ("size", E.string(Size.toString(order.size))),
   ("sleeve", E.string(Sleeve.toString(order.sleeve))),
   ("color", E.string(Color.toString(order.color))),
   ("pattern", E.string(Pattern.toString(order.pattern)))
   ])
  };
  let decodeJson = (json: Js.Json.t): t => {
    {
      orderNumber: D.field("orderNumber", D.int, json),
      quantity: D.field("quantity", D.int, json),
➤     size: Size.decodeJson(D.field("size", D.string, json)),
➤     sleeve: Sleeve.decodeJson(D.field("sleeve", D.string, json)),
➤     color: Color.decodeJson(D.field("color", D.string, json)),
➤     pattern: Pattern.decodeJson(D.field("pattern", D.string, json))
    }
  }
};
```

You may have noticed something else new: calls to decodeJson() for the Size, Sleeve, Color, and Pattern types (the highlighted lines in the preceding code). We need these because the fromString() functions we already have return an option type, and we want the value. Here's the code we add to Size.decodeJson():

reason-react/shirt-storage/src/Shirt.re
```
exception InvalidSize;

let decodeJson = (str: string): t =>
  switch (fromString(str)) {
    | Some(size) => size
    | None => raise(InvalidSize)
  };
```

In keeping with the way the rest of bs-json works, this code raises an exception if we can't convert the string to our desired type. As an added bonus, it declares its own new exception type.

Storing and Retrieving the State

We'll use the browser's localStorage[12] to store the application state. Our code uses these Dom.Storage functions: setItem() takes a key, value, and the localStorage and returns unit. getItem() takes a key and localStorage and returns an option(string): Some(value), or None if the key was not found.

We need to be able to encode and decode the application state as JSON. There's not much new in this code, but I'm presenting it here for completeness:

```
reason-react/shirt-storage/src/OrderForm.re
let encodeState = (s: state): Js.Json.t => {
  Json.Encode.object_([
    ("qtyStr", Json.Encode.string(s.qtyStr)),
    ("sizeStr", Json.Encode.string(s.sizeStr)),
    ("sleeveStr", Json.Encode.string(s.sleeveStr)),
    ("colorStr", Json.Encode.string(s.colorStr)),
    ("patternStr", Json.Encode.string(s.patternStr)),
    ("nextOrderNumber", Json.Encode.int(s.nextOrderNumber)),
    ("orders", Json.Encode.array(Shirt.Order.encodeJson, s.orders)),
    ("errorText", Json.Encode.string(s.errorText)),
    ("editingNumber", switch (s.editingNumber) {
      | Some(n) => Json.Encode.int(n)
      | None => Json.Encode.int(-1)
      })
  ]);
};

let decodeState = (json: Js.Json.t): state => {
  {
    qtyStr: Json.Decode.field("qtyStr", Json.Decode.string, json),
    sizeStr: Json.Decode.field("sizeStr", Json.Decode.string, json),
    sleeveStr: Json.Decode.field("sleeveStr", Json.Decode.string, json),
    colorStr: Json.Decode.field("colorStr", Json.Decode.string, json),
    patternStr: Json.Decode.field("patternStr", Json.Decode.string, json),
    nextOrderNumber: Json.Decode.field("nextOrderNumber", Json.Decode.int, json),
    orders: Json.Decode.field("orders",
      Json.Decode.array(Shirt.Order.decodeJson), json),
    errorText: Json.Decode.field("errorText", Json.Decode.string, json),
    editingNumber: {
      let optN = (Json.Decode.field("editingNumber", Json.Decode.int, json));
      switch (optN) {
        | -1 => None
        | n => Some(n)
      }
    }
  }
};
```

---

12. developer.mozilla.org/en-US/docs/Web/API/Web_Storage_API/Using_the_Web_Storage_API

Here's the code for storing the application state using encodeState():

reason-react/shirt-storage/src/OrderForm.re
```
let localStorageKey = "shirt-orders";

let storeStateLocally = theState => {
  let jsState = encodeState(theState);
  Dom.Storage.setItem(localStorageKey,
    Js.Json.stringify(jsState), Dom.Storage.localStorage);
};
```

Retrieving the state is a bit more involved. The first time someone uses the page, localStorage has no value corresponding to the key. When there is a value, there's no guarantee that it's valid JSON. Our code has to create a "neutral" state to return if either of these situations occurs:

reason-react/shirt-storage/src/OrderForm.re
```
let getStoredState = () => {
  let neutralState: state = {
    qtyStr: "",
    sizeStr: "",
    sleeveStr: "",
    colorStr: "",
    patternStr: "",
    orders: [| |],
    nextOrderNumber: 1,
    errorText: "",
    editingNumber: None
  };
  let optItem = Dom.Storage.getItem(localStorageKey,
    Dom.Storage.localStorage);
  switch (optItem) {
    | Some(jsonStr) =>
        switch (Js.Json.parseExn(jsonStr)) {
          | result => decodeState(result)
          | exception(_) => neutralState
        }
    | None => neutralState
  }
};
```

Now that we know *how* to store and retrieve state, the question is *where* does it go in our code? Let's do the easier one first: figuring out where to call the code to retrieve the state. This involves a change to setting the initial state:

```
initialState: () => getStoredState(),
```

We have to store the state whenever adding, updating, or deleting an order. Instead of using ReasonReact.Update(), we'll use ReasonReact.UpdateWithSideEffects(), and that takes a bit of explaining.

In the previous versions of our program, the reducer property has been a pure function. Pure functions return the same output for the same input, and they don't depend on or change any variables outside their own scope. This is very advantageous for writing programs that are concurrent—when one part of the program can proceed without waiting for another part to finish. However, when we're doing input and output (such as writing and reading local storage), our functions are no longer pure. Imagine two different components on a web page trying to write to the same key in local storage simultaneously. Hilarity ensues.

In order to tell React that we're not only updating the component but also doing side effects, we must call UpdateWithSideEffects(), which takes as its arguments the new state and a function that performs side effects. The state update happens first, *then* the side-effect function, and then the component rendering. Here's the code for adding and deleting entries. The highlighted lines show the changes:

```
reason-react/shirt-storage/src/OrderForm.re
| Enter(order) => {
    let n = Belt.Option.getWithDefault(toInt(state.qtyStr), 0);
    if (n > 0 && n <= 100) {
➤     ReasonReact.UpdateWithSideEffects({
        /* clear out the form fields */
        qtyStr: "",
        sizeStr: "",
        sleeveStr: "",
        colorStr: "",
        patternStr: "",
        orders: switch (state.editingNumber) {
          | Some(n) => Belt.Array.map(state.orders,
            (item) => {(item.orderNumber == n) ? order : item})
          | None => Belt.Array.concat(state.orders, [|order|])
        },
        nextOrderNumber: state.nextOrderNumber + 1,
        editingNumber: None,
        errorText: ""
      },
➤     (self) => storeStateLocally(self.state));
| Delete(order) => {
➤   ReasonReact.UpdateWithSideEffects({
      ...state,
      orders: Belt.Array.keep(state.orders,
        (item) => (item.orderNumber != order.orderNumber))},
➤     (self) => storeStateLocally(self.state))
  }
```

When we click the Update button on an existing order, the local storage doesn't need to change, so that code still uses plain ReasonReact.Update().

Concurrency and React

 As of this writing, React doesn't use any concurrency features, so we *could* get away with using Update() everywhere. However, work is proceeding on React Fiber, which will allow concurrency.

It's Your Turn

First, maybe you *do* want to store the state when people edit an order. Add the appropriate code to make that happen.

Second (and this will be a much more involved project), as we suggested at the start of the chapter, revise the preceding chapter's graphic example on page 138 to use a FrequencyChart component, where the Chart.t object is part of the component rather than a global variable.

Note: I haven't included solutions in the code directory for either of these, but you are ready to tackle these on your own.

Summing Up

You've learned the basics of ReasonReact, and now you can create a simple single-page web application. There's a lot more to React and ReasonReact, but that goes beyond the scope of this book. For the full ReasonReact documentation, see the web site.[13]

And, congratulations! You now know enough ReasonML to be dangerous. You can read Appendix 2, Miscellaneous Topics, on page 173 to find out about some more advanced topics as well as get filled in on some important topics that didn't quite fit elsewhere in the book.

At this point, it's time to let you take the wheel and drive. What direction should you go? Here are some suggestions:

- Rewrite one of your existing programs in ReasonML.

- Start a new, fun project and write it in ReasonML.

- If you would like to introduce ReasonML at your workplace, write a useful tool in ReasonML.

---

13. reasonml.github.io/reason-react/

- Rewrite a non-mission-critical section of your current product in ReasonML as a proof of concept.

Don't be surprised or discouraged if it takes you three or four times as long to write a "simple" program as it would in your favorite programming language. You're learning new concepts and new patterns at the same time you're solving the original programming problem.

Resources are available to you if you get stuck on a problem. Although this book isn't a reference book, you can use it to find similar code examples. The Articles and Videos page at the ReasonML site has links to advanced topics,[14] and the Community page[15] provides ways for you to get in contact with other ReasonML users. I think you'll find the ReasonML community to be quite friendly and welcoming.

That's all I have to say for this book, except a very large thank you for reading it. My hope is that you will have a lot of fun and success in your endeavors with ReasonML.

---

14. reasonml.github.io/docs/en/articles-and-videos#pro-links
15. reasonml.github.io/docs/en/community

Understanding the ReasonML Ecosystem

ReasonML is a new language—and it isn't. In fact, ReasonML belongs to an ecosystem of languages and tools, and this appendix gives you a brief introduction to that ecosystem. Here's a view of that ecosystem, based on a diagram by Dr. Axel Rauschmayer:

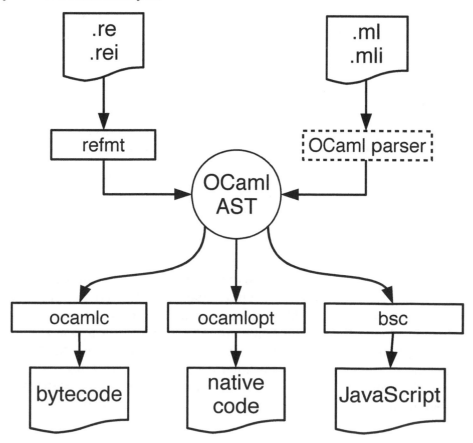

In the Beginning was OCaml

The OCaml language has been in development for over 20 years.[1] (The *ml* in OCaml and in ReasonML stands for *meta-language*, not *machine learning*. The latter abbreviation has become very popular recently and is now a source of some confusion when talking about ReasonML.) Files written in OCaml have an extension of .ml for source code and .mli for interface files. The OCaml parser takes those files to create an internal format known as the OCaml *AST* (Abstract Syntax Tree). The parser is not an independent tool. It is built into the ocamlc, ocamlopt, and bsc tools. Let's talk about them.

The ocamlc compiler translates the AST to a bytecode executable. This bytecode format, like Java bytecode, is intended to be portable. Any system that provides a bytecode interpreter (using the ocamlrun tool, not shown in the diagram) can run a bytecode file. If you need to compile to native code, you use the ocamlopt tool, which outputs code that can directly execute on your operating system. Finally, if you need to compile to JavaScript, you use the bsc (BuckleScript compiler) tool. This modular system is very clever. Anything that produces a valid AST can be compiled to bytecode, native code, or JavaScript.

Enter ReasonML

OCaml is a great language. It has strong typing, an excellent type inference language, features that encourage functional programming, and the ability to do object-oriented programming if that's your preference. Why is OCaml one of the best languages you've never heard of? What's not to like?

The syntax. OCaml's syntax doesn't look like the syntax of many commonly used languages. For example, you don't use parentheses around a function's arguments. You just put them after the function name, separated by whitespace:

```
let average a b = (a +. b) /. 2.0
let result = average 3.0 4.5
```

People often cite OCaml's unusual syntax as a reason for not wanting to learn or adopt the language. Some people at Facebook decided to make a new syntax for OCaml that would be more familiar to JavaScript programmers, so they developed ReasonML. Remember, ReasonML isn't a new language. It's a new *syntax* for OCaml. The bsrefmt tool takes your ReasonML files (with extensions .re for source and .rei for interface files) and translates them to the OCaml AST. Once in that format, your programs are full citizens of the OCaml ecosystem and can take advantage of other code that is written in OCaml.

---

1. ocaml.org/learn/history.html

There's no law that you can't create other syntaxes that compile to the OCaml AST—someone has even written a Lisp-style syntax for OCaml.[2]

Joe asks:
Do I need to know OCaml?

No, you don't *need* to learn it, but it is useful to familiarize yourself with the basics of OCaml syntax. That's because the documentation of the Belt library has all its example code written in OCaml format. I would recommend reading the first chapters of *Real World OCaml*[a] for a good introduction.

If you are faced with an existing OCaml file, you can use the bsrefmt command to convert it to ReasonML:

```
bsrefmt --print=re unfamiliar.ml > familiar.re
```

a. dev.realworldocaml.org/

A Non-Unified Ecosystem

The ReasonML system is not completely unified. For example, the sketch.sh website lets you enter scripts and see them executed immediately. Its back end uses native code—as of this writing, it can't use the Js library, which is tied to the JavaScript world, or the Belt library, which is a standard library shipped with BuckleScript that is also tied to the JavaScript world. On the other hand, the "try it" option at reasonml.github.io/en/try.html lives in the Buckle-Script world and allows you to use both Js and Belt.

There are also differences between BuckleScript and native OCaml, which you may see summarized at bucklescript.github.io/docs/en/difference-from-native-ocaml. Native and JavaScript are two different worlds, and bridging them is a difficult task. Also, as of this writing, you have to ship bs-platform as a dependency if you wish to create an npm package that contains ReasonML/BuckleScript code, though people are working on solving that problem.

Summing Up

ReasonML provides programmers who know JavaScript with a new, more familiar syntax for OCaml. Code written in ReasonML can fit nicely into the existing OCaml system. You can compile ReasonML to portable bytecode, native code, or JavaScript, with the features available to you dependent on the platform you choose.

---

2. github.com/jaredly/myntax

Miscellaneous Topics

We've covered the basics of ReasonML, and you know enough to write simple single-page applications with and without React. In this appendix, we're going to cover some miscellaneous topics that are useful but didn't fit anywhere else in the book. We'll also dive into one advanced topic: hiding type information.

Switching to fun

If you have a function that consists solely of a switch expression, you can write it using the keyword fun without needing to give a parameter. The following two functions do the same thing:

miscellanea/misc/src/Shortcuts.re
```
let recip1 = (x: float): option(float) =>
  switch (x) {
    | 0.0 => None
    | x => Some(1.0 /. x)
  };

let recip2 = fun
  | 0.0 => None
  | x => Some(1.0 /. x);
```

This only works if the switch expression is a simple variable. You can't convert the following switch to fun:

miscellanea/misc/src/Shortcuts.re
```
let toFloat = (s:string): option(float) => {
  switch (float_of_string(s)) {
    | result => Some(result)
    | exception(Failure("float_of_string")) => None
  }
};
```

Using open

Consider this code, which is similar to what we saw in Using Pipe First, on page 44:

miscellanea/misc/src/NoOpen.re

```
let toFloat = (s:string): option(float) => {
  switch (float_of_string(s)) {
    | result => Some(result)
    | exception(Failure("float_of_string")) => None
  }
};

let reciprocal = fun
  | 0.0 => None
  | x => Some(1.0 /. x);

let cube = (x) => x *. x *. x;

let makeDisplayText = fun
    | Some(value) => "The result is " ++ value
    | None => "Could not calculate result.";

let calculation = (input: string): string => {
  toFloat(input)
  -> Belt.Option.flatMap(reciprocal)
  -> Belt.Option.map(cube)
  -> Belt.Option.map(Js.Float.toFixedWithPrecision(~digits=3))
  -> makeDisplayText
};

let cubeArray = (data: array(float)): array(float) => {
  Belt.Array.map(data, cube);
}

Js.log(calculation("0.125"));
Js.log(cubeArray([|3.0, 4.0, 5.0|]));
```

Look at all those calls to Belt.Option. Wouldn't it be nice if we didn't have to type it repeatedly, especially if we had many more functions, *all* using Belt.Option? The solution to this problem is open. If you place an open followed by the module name at the top of your source file, the functions in the opened module are made visible in your module (only the relevant portion is shown here):

miscellanea/misc/src/FullOpen.re

```
let calculation = (input: string): string => {
  toFloat(input)
  -> flatMap(reciprocal)
  -> map(cube)
```

```
    -> map(Js.Float.toFixedWithPrecision(~digits=3))
    -> makeDisplayText
};

let cubeArray = (data: array(float)): array(float) => {
  Belt.Array.map(data, cube);
}
```

You should be cautious when you're doing a full open, especially if you're opening multiple modules. For example, if we were to do the following opens, we would run into trouble because both modules contain a map() function:

```
open Belt.Option;
open Belt.Array;
```

Instead of doing an open for the entire file, you can open a module in a local scope:

miscellanea/misc/src/LocalOpen.re
```
let calculation = (input: string): string => {
  open Belt.Option;
  toFloat(input)
  -> flatMap(reciprocal)
  -> map(cube)
  -> map(Js.Float.toFixedWithPrecision(~digits=3))
  -> makeDisplayText
};

let cubeArray = (data: array(float)): array(float) => {
  open Belt.Array;
  map(data, cube);
}
```

Using Belt.Map.update()

Back in our discussion of Belt.Map on page 115, we updated a map of the color counts by using Belt.Map.getWithDefault() and Belt.Map.set(). While this works, you may find it more convenient to use Belt.Map.update(). This function takes as its parameters the map to be updated, a key, and a function. It works as follows:

- Attempt to get the value for the given key using Belt.Map.get(). This returns an option. If the value is None, the key isn't in the map, so return the map unchanged.

- Otherwise, apply the function to the value. If the function returns None, return a map with the key and value removed.

- If the function returns Some(value), then return an updated map where the value for the given key is value.

Let's look at a concrete example:

miscellanea/misc/src/MapUpdate.re

```
let sickDays = Belt.Map.String.fromArray([|
  ("David", 4),
  ("Cathy", 2), ("Felipe", 1)|]);

let outSick = fun
  | Some(n) => Some(n + 1)
  | None => Some(1);

let remove = (_days: option(int)): option(int) =>  None;

let result1 = Belt.Map.String.update(sickDays, "Cathy", outSick);
/* ("David", 4) ("Cathy", 3) ("Felipe", 1) */

let result2 = Belt.Map.String.update(sickDays, "Joe", outSick);
/* ("David", 4) ("Cathy", 2) ("Felipe", 1) ("Joe", 1) */

let result3 = Belt.Map.String.update(sickDays, "David", remove);
/* ("Cathy", 2) ("Felipe", 1) */

let result4 = Belt.Map.String.update(sickDays, "Paracelsus", remove);
/* ("David", 4) ("Cathy", 2) ("Felipe", 1) */

Js.log2("r1: ", result1);
Js.log2("r2: ", result2);
Js.log2("r3: ", result3);
Js.log2("r4: ", result4);
```

In this example, we're using the Belt.Map.String module, which is optimized for maps with strings as keys. Starting in line 1, we create a map from an array of key-value tuples.

The outSick() function in line 5 has as its input the number of available sick days for a person. If Some(n), we return the updated value Some(n+1). If the person has no sick days, this must be a new entry, thus that person has one sick day.

The remove() function in line 9 always returns None.

Here are the results of several applications of Update(). In the first example on line 11, Cathy is in the map, so her value Some(2) is passed to outSick(), which returns Some(3). The resulting new map is shown as key-value pairs in the next line.

In the next example, Joe is not in the map, so None is passed to outSick(), which returns Some(1). The key "Joe" is added to the map with a value of 1. Notice that Cathy has two sick days—the original sickDays map never gets changed. Belt.Map.Update() always returns a new map.

In the third example, David is in the map, so his value Some(4) is passed to remove(), which returns None. This tells Update() to remove the key "David" with its value of 4.

In the last example, Paracelsus isn't in the map, so remove() never gets called at all, and the new map is identical to the original one.

Dangerous Interop

Sometimes you need to convert a JavaScript type to a ReasonML type. For example, one of the reviewers of this book suggested using the Performance[1] interface for measuring the time required to process the palindrome functions rather than using Js.Date.now() as we did on page 94. He wrote this code:

```
miscellanea/misc/src/Identity.re
module Performance = {
  type t; /* DOMHighResTimeStamp - a double, milliseconds since startup */

  [@bs.scope "performance"] [@bs.module "perf_hooks"]
  external now: unit => t = "";

  external toFloat: t => float = "%identity";
  external fromFloat: float => t = "%identity";

  let zero: t = fromFloat(0.0);

  let addInterval: (t, t, t) => t =
    (current, start, finish) =>
      (toFloat(finish) -. toFloat(start) +. toFloat(current))->fromFloat;
};
```

The JavaScript Performance interface returns a DOMHighResTimeStamp when you call its now() method. We need to be able to treat these values as a ReasonML float. We do this on lines 7 and 8 with "%identity", which is a special escape hatch designed for exactly these cases.[2] One such case is the unsafeAsHtmlElement() function we saw on page 53, which uses %identity to accomplish its task.

If you like to live dangerously—very dangerously—you can use Obj.magic(), which lets you put any sort of value in any context you wish. ReasonML's type checking will close its eyes, take a deep breath, and do your bidding. Whatever happens as a result is on you.

```
miscellanea/misc/src/Magic.re
let x = (Obj.magic(27)) + (Obj.magic(37.5)); /* 64 */
let y = Obj.magic("car") ++ Obj.magic(54);   /* car54 */
```

---

1. developer.mozilla.org/en-US/docs/Web/API/Performance
2. bucklescript.github.io/docs/en/intro-to-external#special-identity-external

Hiding Type Information

Consider this short module that defines a "time of day" type as a record with fields for the hour and minute:

miscellanea/misc/src/RegularType.re

```
/* Interface */
module type Time {
  type t = {
    hour: int,
    minute:int
  };

  let make: (int, int) => t;
  let add: (t, t) => t;
};

/* Implementation */
module Time: Time = {
  type t = {
    hour: int,
    minute:int
  };

  let make = (h:int, m:int): t => {
    {hour: abs(h) mod 24,
      minute: abs(m) mod 60}
  }

  let add = (t1: t, t2: t): t => {
    let total = (t1.hour * 60 + t1.minute) +
      (t2.hour * 60 + t2.minute);
    make(total / 60, total mod 60)
  }
};
```

Let's look at the usage of this module:

miscellanea/misc/src/RegularType.re

```
Line 1  let time1: Time.t = Time.make(15, 30);
   -    Js.log(time1); /* [15, 30] */

   -    let time2: Time.t = {hour: 20, minute: 45};
   5    Js.log(time2); /* [20, 45] */

   -    let time3 = Time.add(time1, time2);
   -    Js.log(time3); /* [12, 15] */

  10    let wrong: Time.t = {hour: -30, minute: 170};
   -    Js.log(wrong); /* [-30, 170] */
```

We can use the make() function to construct a Time.t as in line 1. We can also directly create a compatible record, as in line 4, and then add time1 and time2.

It's all fun and games until someone creates a Time.t with invalid values in line 10.

ReasonML lets you hide information about your types so that the *only* way they can create a valid value is through the functions in your module. We accomplish this by making the type abstract:

miscellanea/misc/src/HiddenType.re
```
/* Interface */
module type Time {
➤   type t;

    let make: (int, int) => t;
    let add: (t, t) => t;
};
```

The highlighted line shows the only change. Now users of our Time module know only that it has a type t, but they have no access to its internal representation. This means that when we try to do a direct assignment—valid or not—such as:

```
let time2: Time.t = {hour:20, minute: 45};
```

ReasonML will complain:

```
We've found a bug for you!
/path/to/code/miscellanea/misc/src/HiddenType.re 35:22-25

33 │ Js.log(time1); /* [15, 30] */
34 │
35 │ let time2: Time.t = {hour: 20, minute: 45};
36 │ Js.log(time2); /* [20, 45] */
37 │

The record field hour can't be found.
```

Using the module correctly with the hidden type now looks like this:

miscellanea/misc/src/HiddenType.re
```
let time1: Time.t = Time.make(15, 30);
Js.log(time1); /* [15, 30] */

let time2: Time.t = Time.make(20, 45);
Js.log(time2); /* [20, 45] */

let time3 = Time.add(time1, time2);
Js.log(time3); /* [12, 15] */

let wrong = Time.make(-30, 170);
Js.log(wrong); /* [6, 50] */
```

We can still give weird numbers to make(). But, since it forces the numbers into a valid range, and our other operations such as add() keep the numbers in range, we never have to worry about someone using our module to generate an impossible time like -30 hours and 170 minutes. It would, of course, be possible to have make() produce option(t) values when given bad input. In fact, that's more in the spirit of ReasonML, but I didn't want to add an extra layer of complexity to this example.

A closely allied concept is *phantom types*, which are parameterized types whose parameters don't appear on the right-hand side of the definition. You can find out more about them at medium.com/reasontraining/phantom-types-in-reasonml-1a4cfc18d999 and gist.github.com/busypeoples/3a28d039272ec3eb33ca2fc6b32dafc7.

Index

Thank you!

How did you enjoy this book? Please let us know. Take a moment and email us at support@pragprog.com with your feedback. Tell us your story and you could win free ebooks. Please use the subject line "Book Feedback."

Ready for your next great Pragmatic Bookshelf book? Come on over to https://pragprog.com and use the coupon code BUYANOTHER2019 to save 30% on your next ebook.

Void where prohibited, restricted, or otherwise unwelcome. Do not use ebooks near water. If rash persists, see a doctor. Doesn't apply to *The Pragmatic Programmer* ebook because it's older than the Pragmatic Bookshelf itself. Side effects may include increased knowledge and skill, increased marketability, and deep satisfaction. Increase dosage regularly.

And thank you for your continued support,

Andy Hunt, Publisher

Programming Elm

Elm brings the safety and stability of functional pro-
graming to front-end development, making it one of
the most popular new languages. Elm's functional na-
ture and static typing means that run-time errors are
nearly impossible, and it compiles to JavaScript for
easy web deployment. This book helps you take advantage of this new language in your web site development.
Learn how the Elm Architecture will help you create
fast applications. Discover how to integrate Elm with
JavaScript so you can update legacy applications. See
how Elm tooling makes deployment quicker and easier.

Jeremy Fairbank
(250 pages) ISBN: 9781680502855. $40.95
https://pragprog.com/book/jfelm

Learn Functional Programming with Elixir

Elixir's straightforward syntax and this guided tour
give you a clean, simple path to learn modern functional programming techniques. No previous functional
programming experience required! This book walks
you through the right concepts at the right pace, as
you explore immutable values and explicit data trans-
formation, functions, modules, recursive functions,
pattern matching, high-order functions, polymorphism,
and failure handling, all while avoiding side effects.
Don't board the Elixir train with an imperative mindset!
To get the most out of functional languages, you need
to think functionally. This book will get you there.

Ulisses Almeida
(198 pages) ISBN: 9781680502459. $42.95
https://pragprog.com/book/cdc-elixir

Programming Clojure, Third Edition

Drowning in unnecessary complexity, unmanaged state, and tangles of spaghetti code? In the best tradition of Lisp, Clojure gets out of your way so you can focus on expressing simple solutions to hard problems. Clojure cuts through complexity by providing a set of composable tools—immutable data, functions, macros, and the interactive REPL. Written by members of the Clojure core team, this book is the essential, definitive guide to Clojure. This new edition includes information on all the newest features of Clojure, such as transducers and specs.

Alex Miller with Stuart Halloway and Aaron Bedra
(302 pages) ISBN: 9781680502466. $49.95
https://pragprog.com/book/shcloj3

Functional Programming in Java

Get ready to program in a whole new way. *Functional Programming in Java* will help you quickly get on top of the new, essential Java 8 language features and the functional style that will change and improve your code. This short, targeted book will help you make the paradigm shift from the old imperative way to a less error-prone, more elegant, and concise coding style that's also a breeze to parallelize. You'll explore the syntax and semantics of lambda expressions, method and constructor references, and functional interfaces. You'll design and write applications better using the new standards in Java 8 and the JDK.

Venkat Subramaniam
(196 pages) ISBN: 9781937785468. $33
https://pragprog.com/book/vsjava8

Practical Security

Most security professionals don't have the words "security" or "hacker" in their job title. Instead, as a developer or admin you often have to fit in security alongside your official responsibilities — building and maintaining computer systems. Implement the basics of good security now, and you'll have a solid foundation if you bring in a dedicated security staff later. Identify the weaknesses in your system, and defend against the attacks most likely to compromise your organization, without needing to become a trained security professional.

Roman Zabicki
(132 pages) ISBN: 9781680506341. $26.95
https://pragprog.com/book/rzsecur

Secure Your Node.js Web Application

Cyber-criminals have your web applications in their crosshairs. They search for and exploit common security mistakes in your web application to steal user data. Learn how you can secure your Node.js applications, database and web server to avoid these security holes. Discover the primary attack vectors against web applications, and implement security best practices and effective countermeasures. Coding securely will make you a stronger web developer and analyst, and you'll protect your users.

Karl Düüna
(230 pages) ISBN: 9781680500851. $36
https://pragprog.com/book/kdnodesec

Small, Sharp Software Tools

The command-line interface is making a comeback. That's because developers know that all the best features of your operating system are hidden behind a user interface designed to help average people use the computer. But you're not the average user, and the CLI is the most efficient way to get work done fast. Turn tedious chores into quick tasks: read and write files, manage complex directory hierarchies, perform network diagnostics, download files, work with APIs, and combine individual programs to create your own workflows. Put down that mouse, open the CLI, and take control of your software development environment.

Brian P. Hogan
(200 pages) ISBN: 9781680502961. $38.95
https://pragprog.com/book/bhcldev

Rediscovering JavaScript

JavaScript is no longer to be feared or loathed—the world's most popular and ubiquitous language has evolved into a respectable language. Whether you're writing frontend applications or server-side code, the phenomenal features from ES6 and beyond—like the rest operator, generators, destructuring, object literals, arrow functions, modern classes, promises, async, and metaprogramming capabilities—will get you excited and eager to program with JavaScript. You've found the right book to get started quickly and dive deep into the essence of modern JavaScript. Learn practical tips to apply the elegant parts of the language and the gotchas to avoid.

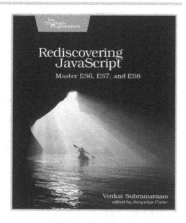

Venkat Subramaniam
(286 pages) ISBN: 9781680505467. $45.95
https://pragprog.com/book/ves6

The Pragmatic Bookshelf

The Pragmatic Bookshelf features books written by developers for developers. The titles continue the well-known Pragmatic Programmer style and continue to garner awards and rave reviews. As development gets more and more difficult, the Pragmatic Programmers will be there with more titles and products to help you stay on top of your game.

Visit Us Online

This Book's Home Page
https://pragprog.com/book/reasonml
Source code from this book, errata, and other resources. Come give us feedback, too!

Keep Up to Date
https://pragprog.com
Join our announcement mailing list (low volume) or follow us on twitter @pragprog for new titles, sales, coupons, hot tips, and more.

New and Noteworthy
https://pragprog.com/news
Check out the latest pragmatic developments, new titles and other offerings.

Save on the eBook

Save on the eBook versions of this title. Owning the paper version of this book entitles you to purchase the electronic versions at a terrific discount.

PDFs are great for carrying around on your laptop—they are hyperlinked, have color, and are fully searchable. Most titles are also available for the iPhone and iPod touch, Amazon Kindle, and other popular e-book readers.

Buy now at *https://pragprog.com/coupon*

Contact Us

Online Orders:	*https://pragprog.com/catalog*
Customer Service:	*support@pragprog.com*
International Rights:	*translations@pragprog.com*
Academic Use:	*academic@pragprog.com*
Write for Us:	*http://write-for-us.pragprog.com*
Or Call:	+1 800-699-7764